The
Shortcut
Cook
All in One

The Shortcut Cook All in One

One-dish recipes and ingenious hacks to make faster and tastier food

Rosie Reynolds

Photography by Clare Winfield

Hardie Grant

BOOKS

For Curt and Auguste

Contents

Introduction

As a trained chef, cookbook author and food stylist I have worked on many cookbooks and written hundreds of recipes. It is my job to get great tasting, beautiful food on the table (or set) usually in a short space of time and under a certain amount of pressure and scrutiny. Over time I have developed plenty of shortcuts to make great meals, faster and easier, that taste delicious and look good without sacrificing flavour, texture or eye appeal. As a mother, I also get to continually practise my skills of cooking for my family at home and, well, sometimes I just need to make it even easier!

My last book, *The Shortcut Cook*, was filled with lots of shortcuts, or 'tricks of the trade'; those things chefs and food professionals just do as part of their daily job without thinking about it or, in some instances, even realising it. Well, I'm here to let you in on more creative solutions, tricks and ingredients that will provide delicious meals that are easy to prepare with depths of flavour and less work in the kitchen for you and your family.

Like *The Shortcut Cook*, this book is intended for home cooks who want a straightforward, practical approach to preparing tasty, beautiful food without pretence. But I've managed to make it even easier. How, you ask? I've cooked everything in just one pan, pot or dish. Super tasty, super stylish, super simple.

This is how I cook for my family to harness and concentrate flavours into one dish that leads to the enjoyment of beautiful delicious food that is easy to prepare. With this book I'd love you to find the enthusiasm that I have for the food I cook and to embrace some of the kitchen wisdom I've learned over the years.

I hope this book inspires you to get into the kitchen and to enjoy the process of cooking a great meal for yourself, friends and family.

Rosie

How the recipes work

I always like to start every cooking journey by reading through the recipe I'm setting out to make. I take notice of the ingredients. Do I have everything? If not, can I make an easy substitution and will the recipe still work? Thinking of swapping chickpeas (garbanzos) for cannellini beans – yes it will! Thinking of swapping flour for chia seeds – no it probably won't!

I read the method before I start cooking not only to see if it is possible at the particular meal time but so I know what is coming up. It's super helpful to read the first couple of lines of the recipe before you skip back to prepping and chopping – if it says 'preheat the oven' you can do this immediately so you are ready to go. In this book you will also see the size and type of cooking vessel you need to use.

You'll see that I have a few favourite ingredients that are always in my cupboard. If you have these on standby, you'll never struggle to put together a tasty meal: olive oil, light-flavoured oil – I use sunflower or rapeseed – garlic, onions, tinned tomatoes, eggs, ginger, bacon, Parmesan, honey, frozen pastry. And a well stocked spice rack containing all the basics including cinnamon, cumin, paprika, garlic granules, turmeric, chilli (hot pepper) flakes, etc.

I love fresh herbs. I keep mine in a glass jar in some water in the refrigerator. Thyme, rosemary and bay leaves will last for ages and are good fresh or dried.

All the recipes have a preparation time (this tells you how long it will take to get everything ready for cooking) and a cook time (how long the recipe will take on the stove or in the oven). These are a guide, so please use them as such.

The ingredients are listed in the order in which they appear in the method, the preparation required is listed next to the ingredient (e.g. sliced, grated, chopped, etc.). If you work your way down the ingredient list and prepare the ingredients as you go, you will be ready to start cooking as soon as you reach the end of the list. There is a fancy chef term for this: mis-en-place (everything in its place).

The 'shortcut' from each recipe is highlighted so you know how this recipe is saving you time, or helping you achieve a more delicious result.

I would urge you to follow the recipes closely the first time you cook them. I have tried and tested the recipes and know they work, taste delicious and look great. Once you've made it, eaten it, talked about it, taken a picture of it, digested it, then you can make it again, putting your stamp on it and making it your own.

General tips

There are some things that I'll always do when I'm cooking, which make my life easier, make cooking more pleasurable and help food taste its best.

Gather everything before you start cooking: equipment, ingredients, a clean dish towel, etc.

Have a large bowl or a plastic bag nearby for food waste, to keep your work station clean and clutter-free.

Fill the sink with hot soapy water to keep your hands clean and to speedily wash up used or dirty bowls and equipment for quick re-use. Keep a clean cloth close by for wiping and some paper towels for patting, drying and draining foods.

Start your cooking sessions by putting on the kettle – this will mean you can make up stock from cubes quickly, rinse out tins to add the liquid to sauces and stews, or get pasta on the boil much quicker.

Most pastas don't need to cook in a huge pot of boiling water, they will cook just as well in a smaller pan. Doing this will also give you an intensely starchy cooking water, which will thicken your sauce with great success. The same goes for boiling vegetables: you don't need huge vats of water to cook veg, just a pan that's fit for purpose.

Make sure meat is not refrigerator-cold when you put it in the oven, as it will take a good 20–30 minutes to warm through before it can start cooking.

Like meat, eggs need to come to room temperature before cooking. This will prevent them curdling cake mixes or being undercooked when boiled.

Sharp knives will speed things up in the kitchen; a speed peeler will thinly and evenly slice; and a good pair of kitchen scissors will snip precisely.

Equipment

The equipment list for this book is, by design, neat and tidy. I use the following tins and trays (pans) to test the recipes in this book, but you can vary the sizes slightly or substitute trays for other tins, but keep your eye on the timings as they may change if you take too much of a wild detour from the size or type of tray specified. For baking I'd suggest sticking to the size listed as I know they will work. I favour metal, ceramic or cast iron to cook with, but if you're confident with silicone and alternative materials that's great. Once again, keep your eye on timings as I don't test my recipes in these alternative materials.

Baking trays/pans/tins

A standard 30 x 20 x 5 cm (12 x 8 x 2 in) enamelware/metal tray (pan):
This size is great when you have sauce and food that needs to be contained as all the flavour is harnessed in the tray.

Large 39 x 27 x 2 cm (15½ x 10 ¾ x ¾ in) metal baking tray:
This size is ideal when you have vegetables that need to char and gain colour while they cook, and the extra space allows the hot air of the oven to circulate so the food cooks all around and prevents steaming the vegetables.

Extra large 37 x 33 x 4 cm (14½ x 13 x 1½ in) metal tray (usually the shelf-cum-tray that comes with the oven):
This is the perfect tray when you need to fit a lot on and you need everything to crisp up. I love cooking fish and chips on this tray.

Ovenproof cast-iron casserole dish with lid (Dutch oven), about 31 cm (12½ in) in diameter (suitable for stovetop and oven):
Perfect when you start a dish on the stove and move it into the oven or flash it under a hot grill (broiler). Such a versatile piece of kit and one I couldn't live without.

900 g (2 lb) loaf pan, about 23 x 13 x 7 cm (9 x 5 x 2¾ in):
This is a standard loaf pan. I make so much in mine, from the Gooey Lemon Bars (page 136) to the No-Churn Strawberry Cheesecake Ice Cream (page 145) to the Roasted Vegetable, Pesto and Ricotta Loaf Pan Lasagne (page 59) .

Other useful equipment

A large sharp knife: A good sharp knife you feel comfortable with will not only speed up your chopping it will make chopping safer as you're far less likely to cut yourself with a sharp knife.

Serrated knife: Great for cutting fruit, bread and cakes. If you don't like using a big sharp knife, consider investing in a good serrated knife; you won't be quick but you will be able to chop!

Mixing bowls: Have a selection to hand.

Digital scales: Use digital scales for accuracy in cooking especially when you are baking.

Set of measuring spoons: For accuracy, have a selection from ¼ teaspoon to 1 tablespoon.

Measuring jug: This is essential for liquids and mixing stock cubes (although if you don't have a set you can also weigh liquid on your digital scales).

Mixing spoons and spatulas: I love my heatproof rubber spatulas and have a big one and a small one. You can buy them from a chefs' supplier and they are super cheap and super rewarding to use. I also have a couple of long-handled wooden spoons, a large metal spoon, a slotted metal spoon, a spatula for flipping and a palette knife for transferring and spreading icing (frosting) and things like that.

Cutting board: I have a large wooden cutting board that sits comfortably on my work surface. It's nothing fancy but it is good quality and heavy, so it doesn't wobble. It is also light enough that I can pick it up as often as necessary to wash it with hot soapy water.

Hand-held electric whisk: Use an electric whisk for whipping and whisking, especially my favourite aquafaba, which is difficult by hand!

Box grater and a precision grater: I use both for so many things and marvel at how fast a lovely sharp precision grater is every time.

Speed vegetable peeler: This makes peeling a pleasure.

Kitchen scissors: Buy a good strong pair and use them for everything from chopping soft vegetables directly into the pan to snipping herbs for a salad.

Rolling pin: These are great for pastry and, my favourite, bashing things into crumbs!

Strong sandwich bags/freezer bags: I use these for everything from bashing biscuits (cookies) into crumbs to packing extra food up for the freezer.

Breakfast and brunch

Apricot breakfast cake with seeded streusel topping

Makes 12 | Prep 15 minutes | Cook 45 minutes

The Shortcut

I use tinned apricots in juice as they are available all year round and a bargain too. If you prefer, use fresh apricots when they are in season and swap with apples or pears for a change.

175 g (6 oz) butter, softened, plus extra for greasing
100 g (3½ oz) light soft brown sugar
50 g (2 oz/¼ cup) Demerara sugar
2 large eggs
100 g (3½ oz) Greek-style yoghurt
150 g (5 oz/scant 1¼ cups) plain (all-purpose) flour
150 g (5 oz/1½ cups) ground almonds
1 teaspoon baking powder
pinch of salt
411 g (14 oz) tin apricot halves, drained and patted dry with paper towels

For the seeded streusel topping
50 g (2 oz) butter, softened
50 g (2 oz/¼ cup) Demerara sugar
75 g (2½ oz/scant ⅔ cup) plain (all-purpose) flour
75 g (2½ oz/⅔ cup) mixed seeds

I have always loved a piece of dense cake for breakfast, and this cake hits all the right spots, as it's moist with ground almonds and yoghurt in the sponge and dotted with juicy apricots. I also love the textural contrast of the crunch from the mixed seed and Demerara streusel topping against the soft apricots and tender crumb. Their delicious toasty flavour, crunch and health benefits make this cake a good choice for breakfast on the go or brunch with friends. This is the easiest of cakes to make, and, if you can resist eating it all, it gets better after a few days. It will keep well for 3–5 days wrapped in baking parchment and stored in an airtight container.

———

Preheat the oven to 160°C fan (325°F/gas 3) and grease and line a 30 x 20 x 5 cm (12 x 8 x 2 in) rectangular baking tin (pan) with baking parchment.

First, make the seeded streusel topping, in a small bowl, rub the butter, sugar and flour together with your fingertips until it is clumping together. Stir in the seeds and squeeze with your fingertips to incorporate until the mixture looks like damp sand. Set aside.

Beat the butter and both sugars together in a large bowl until creamy. Add the eggs, beating after each addition until combined. Add the yoghurt and beat again, then add the flour, ground almonds, baking powder and salt. Stir the mixture until it is a thick, smooth cake batter.

Transfer the cake batter to the prepared tin, spreading it out into an even layer. Dot the apricot halves over the surface, then sprinkle the streusel topping evenly over the top. There will be some parts of the apricots and cake batter poking through, but don't worry, this makes the texture even more intriguing and the cake prettier.

Bake in the oven for 45 minutes, or until a skewer inserted into the centre of the cake comes out clean. Leave to cool in the tin for 15 minutes, then transfer to a cutting board and cut into squares. Serve warm or leave to cool completely, then wrap and store in an airtight container for up to 5 days.

Za'atar and feta croissants

Makes 6 | Prep 15 minutes | Cook 20 minutes

The Shortcut

I use good-quality ready-rolled puff pastry. A ruler (or straight edge) and a sharp knife will help you cut the pastry neatly, giving the most professional result.

320 g (11 oz) packet ready-rolled puff pastry (I love Dorset pastry)
1 egg, lightly beaten
2 tablespoons za'atar
75 g (2½ oz) grated mozzarella
80 g (3 oz) feta

I will be straight with you: I have what can only be described as a pastry problem. I am totally addicted and cannot resist a good flavour combination. This Middle Eastern-inspired flavour mix works so well; traditionally sprinkled on manakish, the Lebanese thin, doughy (addictive) flatbread, I decided to use it in my other personal favourite – buttery, flaky, crisp puff pastry. The sharp feta, zingy sumac in the za'atar and the oozy mozzarella are delicious served with boiled eggs for brunch.

———

Preheat the oven to 180°C fan (350°F/gas 4) and line a flat baking sheet with baking parchment.

Unroll the dough but keep it on the wrapping paper, then use a large sharp knife to cut it into three equal rectangles, about 12 cm (4½ in) across and 22 cm (8½ in) tall. Cut each rectangle into triangles, starting from one corner and cutting diagonally to the opposite corner to create two long right-angled triangles.

Brush the surface of the triangles lightly with some of the beaten egg, then scatter over 1½ tablespoons of za'atar and the mozzarella, gently pressing it in with your hands so that it sticks.

Divide the feta into six pieces, then take one portion and crumble it along the base of one triangle. Slowly roll the pastry upwards to the point of the triangle. Transfer to the baking sheet, pushing in any stray bits of cheese. Don't worry too much about this as any escapees will crisp up and only add to the taste and texture of your finished pastries.

Repeat this step with the remaining feta and pastry to form more croissants. Brush each pastry with the remaining beaten egg and sprinkle over the remaining za'atar. Bake in the oven for 15–20 minutes until golden brown.

Tip If you can't find za'atar, mix 1 tablespoon each of sumac, dried thyme, dried oregano, toasted sesame seeds together. Leftovers can be stored in a jar.

Sausage, egg and cheese breakfast rolls

Serves 6 | Prep 15 minutes | Cook 35 minutes

The Shortcut

Making a loaded frittata with sausage, cheese and fluffy eggs is so much easier than cooking everything individually, and the beauty of this is that all the flavours get to cook together resulting in an even more delicious sandwich.

6 good-quality pork or chicken
   sausages
pinch of chilli (hot pepper) flakes
8 large eggs, lightly beaten
100 g (3½ oz) strong Cheddar,
   grated
salt and freshly ground black
   pepper
6 English muffins or crusty rolls, split
2 large handfuls mixed leaves
   (I used watercress, rocket and
   spinach)

For the spicy sauce (optional)
4 tablespoons tomato ketchup
2 tablespoons sriracha sauce
3 tablespoons mayonnaise

When I need something comforting and deeply satisfying, I always opt for a breakfast roll, and while I love them I don't always feel like making them – sometimes the logistics feel like too much hard work! This sandwich is basically a sausage frittata filled with all the good stuff. It's so good, you have to tray it (ha, sorry, try it). I like to serve my sausage and egg rolls with a spicy sauce as it brings all the flavours together so well and helps to stick the rolls together, so the contents of your roll stay where they're supposed to and not down your front – perfect really!

———

Preheat the oven to 160°C fan (325°F/gas 3) and line a 30 x 20 x 5 cm (12 x 8 x 2 in) baking tray (pan) with baking parchment.

Squeeze the sausages out of their skins directly into the prepared tray, breaking up any large chunks so you have even-size sausage pieces. Sprinkle over the chilli flakes and bake in the oven for 15 minutes, or until cooked through and starting to take on some colour. Remove from the oven and leave to cool slightly.

Meanwhile, in a jug, beat the eggs, grated Cheddar and plenty of seasoning together. Stir the sausages in the tray, making sure they are evenly spread out, then pour the egg mixture over the top. Bake for 20 minutes, or until set and golden.

Toast the muffins in a toaster or put directly on the oven shelf below the eggs for the last 2 minutes of cooking. Mix all the ingredients for the spicy sauce (if using) together in a bowl.

To serve, spread a little of the spicy sauce (if using) on the top and bottom halves of the muffins. Cut the sausage and egg into 6 squares, then pop one square on to each muffins bottom, add some mixed leaves and sandwich with the top half of the muffins. Eat immediately.

Tip If you have some leftover sausages, cut them into slices and go straight to step 3 in the recipe.

Saucy tomato baked beans with eggs

Serves 2–4 | Prep 10 minutes | Cook 40 minutes

The Shortcut

Roasting everything together in a tray (pan) means you can just forget about it and let it do its thing. Don't rinse your beans as the liquid from the tin helps to make a delicious rich, velvety sauce that clings to the beans.

1 small red onion, cut into thin wedges through the root
1 red (bell) pepper, sliced
12 cherry tomatoes, halved
2 tablespoons olive oil, plus extra for drizzling
½–1 teaspoon chilli (hot pepper) flakes (depending on how spicy you like it)
400 g (14 oz) tin cannellini beans
200 g (7 oz) carton passata (sieved tomatoes)
1 teaspoon red wine vinegar
4 eggs
small handful of flat-leaf parsley, finely chopped
small handful of dill, finely chopped
salt and freshly ground black pepper

To serve
200 g (7 oz) Greek-style yoghurt and ½ crushed garlic clove stirred in (optional)
lots of buttered toast

I have never met a tomato-sauced bean I didn't like, and these are a particular favourite. So simple to make and great for a quick, healthy but stylish brunch. I like to serve these with a dollop of garlicky yoghurt and buttered toast. It's super simple and delicious.

———

Preheat the oven to 180°C fan (350°F/gas 4).

Put the onion wedges, sliced pepper and cherry tomatoes into a 30 x 20 x 5 cm (12 x 8 x 2 in) roasting tin (pan). Pour over the olive oil, chilli flakes and plenty of seasoning and toss to coat. Roast in the oven for 20 minutes.

Remove the tray from the oven, stir in the beans (and the liquid from the tin), the passata and vinegar, then return to the oven and cook for a further 10 minutes.

Remove the tray from the oven and use a spoon to form four wells in the beans. Crack an egg into each well, then return to the oven and cook for 6–10 minutes until the eggs are cooked to your liking. Scatter over the herbs and a drizzle of oil and serve immediately with garlic yoghurt (if you like) and buttered toast for dunking.

Tip Make this vegan by leaving out the eggs as the beans are delicious on toast with a drizzle of oil. Swap out the dairy yoghurt for your favourite alternative.

Crispy hash browns with bacon, avocado and roasted tomatoes

Serves 4 | Prep 20 minutes | Cook 20 minutes

The Shortcut

Giving the potatoes a quick blast in the microwave helps to hold the hash browns together. Don't peel the potatoes as the skin adds a great taste. As the bacon cooks its fat adds flavour to the hash browns and helps to make the edges crispy.

4 (about 200 g/7 oz each) floury potatoes, left whole
1 teaspoon cornflour (cornstarch)
salt and freshly ground black pepper
2 tablespoons lightly flavoured oil
8 rashers (slices) smoky bacon
25 g (1 oz) butter
200 g (7 oz) vine-ripened tomatoes, snipped into small bunches
4 eggs (optional)

To serve

1 large ripe avocado, halved, stoned (pitted) and flesh scooped out
chilli jam (optional)

I love the unforced celebratory nature of brunch and recipes like this one are so effortless as they allow you to sit and enjoy the moment as much as the food.

———

Preheat the oven to 180°C fan (350°F/gas 4).

Prick the potatoes all over with a fork, then cook in the microwave on full power for 6 minutes, turning over halfway through until the potatoes are just starting to soften. Remove and set aside until cool enough to handle.

Coarsely grate the potatoes into a bowl. Keep any potato skin that gathers, roughly chop it and add it to the grated potato. Add the cornflour and season really well. Divide the potato mixture into 4 equal portions.

Add 2 tablespoons of oil to a large 39 x 32 x 2 cm (15½ x 12½ x ¾ in) baking tray (pan) and heat in the oven for 3 minutes. Remove the hot tray and carefully add the potatoes to the tray, forming it into four scraggly edged circles, about 10 cm (4 in) across and 1 cm (½ in) high. Spoon a little fat from the tray over each one. Add the bacon to the tray and cook in the oven for 10 minutes, or until turning golden at the edges.

Remove the tray from the oven, flip the hash browns over and dot the tomatoes around. Make some space and crack the eggs (if using) into the tray. You can also make a well in your hash browns to crack the eggs in if you prefer. Cook for 4–6 minutes until the tomatoes are softened and the eggs are cooked to your liking. Serve with avocado and chilli jam, if you like.

Tip This is also delicious with smoked salmon and a dollop of cream cheese.

No-knead focaccia with cherry tomatoes and whipped goat's cheese

Serves 4 with leftovers | Prep 20 minutes, plus resting | Cook 20 minutes

The Shortcut

Just give the ingredients a stir, then leave the dish to do its thing. Use your hands to mix the dough as it's much easier... what washing-up?

This bread is sublime and is made even better by the fact you don't have to knead it; a quick mix and a long slow rise is all it takes. The dough rises for 12 hours making it the perfect project to start the night before you plan on serving it.

---

500 g (1 lb 2 oz/4 cups) strong white bread flour
½ x 7 g (¼ oz) sachet fast-action dried yeast
400 ml (13 fl oz/generous 1½ cups) tepid water
2 teaspoons fine sea salt, plus flaky salt to sprinkle
4 tablespoons olive oil, plus extra for rubbing
1 tablespoon cold water

For the whipped goat's cheese
150 g (5 oz) soft goat's cheese
salt and freshly ground black pepper
150 g (5 oz) Greek-style yoghurt
½ garlic clove, crushed
olive oil, for drizzling

For the cherry tomato salad (optional)
200 g (7 oz) cherry tomatoes, halved
½ garlic clove, grated
1 tablespoon red wine vinegar

Put the flour and yeast into a large bowl. In a large jug, stir the tepid water and salt together until dissolved.

Pour the salt water into the flour with 1 tablespoon of olive oil and mix until fully combined and there are no lumps of flour. Rub a little extra oil over the surface of the dough, cover with a clean, damp dish towel and leave somewhere cool (not cold) for 10 hours to double in size.

For the whipped goat's cheese, beat the goat's cheese in a bowl until smooth. Season. Stir in the yoghurt and garlic. Drizzle over olive oil, cover and chill until required.

Add 2 tablespoons oil to a 30 x 20 x 5 cm (12 x 8 x 2 in) baking tray (pan). Tip the dough into the prepared tray and pull the dough's edge furthest from you up and over the dough. Rotate the tray through 90 degrees and repeat this by bringing the dough up and over the dough in the tray. Repeat until you have turned the tray through a full 360 degrees. Cover with the damp dish towel and leave to rest in the refrigerator for 2 hours.

Remove the dough from the refrigerator and use your fingertips to push the dough into an even layer. Dimple the surface with your fingertips and leave to stand while you preheat the oven to 220°C fan (425°F/gas 7).

In a small bowl, whisk the remaining 1 tablespoon of olive oil with the cold water until emulsified. Pour over the dough and sprinkle generously with flaky salt.

Open the oven door and place the tray on the shelf, then quickly throw in a cup of ice-cold water and shut the door to trap the steam created. Bake for 20–25 minutes until the dough is golden and bubbled up. Remove from the oven and leave to cool for 10 minutes, then transfer to a wire rack to cool to room temperature. Slice and serve with the whipped goat's cheese and a tomato salad (if you like) dressed with olive oil, garlic and vinegar.

Spiced potatoes with cracked eggs

Serves 4 | Prep 15 minutes | Cook 30 minutes

The Shortcut

Don't bother peeling the potatoes as the skin adds a lovely texture and nutty flavour. I love cracking eggs straight into the potatoes, as they get covered in some of the spices, and you are not using lots of pans so there's less to wash up. If there are only two of us for brunch, then I serve it straight from the tray (pan).

2 tablespoons lightly flavoured oil
4 potatoes, cut into 2 cm (¾ in) cubes
2 red onions, cut into wedges through the root
½ teaspoon turmeric
1 teaspoon cumin seeds
1 teaspoon paprika
1 teaspoon garlic granules
salt and freshly ground black pepper
4 large eggs
30 g (1 oz) coriander (cilantro) sprigs, stems finely chopped, leaves whole
1 green chilli, finely chopped
4 tablespoons plain yoghurt
4 tablespoons mango chutney
soft white naan bread or toast, to serve

I absolutely love these crunchy potatoes with soft, fluffy centres and bright yellow, runny eggs. It's reminiscent of Indian chaat with its multiple textures and sweet, spicy, sour flavour notes and, of course, a crispy potato hash. Feel free to add sausage or halloumi, chopped bacon or even a tin of chickpeas – anything goes in this delicious recipe.

———

Preheat the oven to 200°C fan (400°F/gas 6).

Carefully the oil into a large 39 x 27 x 2 cm (15½ x 10¾ x ¾ in) baking tray (pan) and heat in the oven for 3 minutes. Remove the tray and carefully add the potatoes and three-quarters of the onion wedges (reserve the final quarter for later). Sprinkle with the turmeric, cumin, paprika, garlic granules and plenty of seasoning and toss to coat. Roast in the oven for 25 minutes, turning the potatoes halfway through with a spatula.

Remove the tray from the oven and make four wells in the potatoes. Crack an egg into each well. Return to the oven and cook for 3–5 minutes until the eggs are cooked to your liking. Check after 3 minutes as the eggs cook quickly.

Gently stir the chopped coriander stems and chilli through the crisp potatoes, dollop yoghurt and chutney over the top and scatter over the coriander leaves and reserved sliced red onions. Serve with soft white naan bread or toast.

Brioche blueberry buns

Makes 4 | Prep 15 minutes | Cook 20 minutes, plus cooling

The Shortcut

No making dough for this one. Use a shop-bought brioche bun and a handful of other simple ingredients to create something totally delicious and beautiful to boot.

4 brioche buns
3 tablespoons caster (superfine) sugar
1 tablespoon soft butter
1 tablespoon plain (all-purpose) flour
½ teaspoon ground cinnamon
2 tablespoons thick Greek-style yoghurt
1 egg
85 g (3 oz) whole (full-fat) cream cheese
1 teaspoon vanilla extract
about 28 blueberries
icing (confectioners') sugar, for dusting

I kept seeing yoghurt toast all over the internet and thinking about how mouthwatering and like custard it looked, which meant I had to try it. I'm partial to a blueberry brioche bun with streusel topping, too, so I thought I'd marry the two and here's what I ended up with. It is utterly delicious and the blueberries and yoghurt – to which I added a dollop of cream cheese – are just the best companion to the buttery brioche. I've also made a streusel topping from the brioche offcuts that crisps up to perfection and adds a great textural contrast to the creamy yoghurt custard and bursting juicy blueberries.

———

Preheat the oven to 160°C fan (325°F/gas 3).

Using a small, sharp, serrated knife, carefully cut a rough 5–6 cm (2–2½ in) circle from each top half of the brioche rolls. Don't go through to the bottom half (you can use a round cutter if you have one). Arrange the buns on a 39 x 27 x 2 cm (15½ x 10¾ x ¾ in) baking tray (pan).

Finely chop the cut-outs and put into a small bowl. Add half the sugar, butter, flour and cinnamon and rub together with your fingertips until the mixture resembles a buttery, sugary rubble. Set aside.

Mix the yoghurt, egg, cream cheese, remaining sugar and vanilla extract together in a small bowl until smooth. Put two blueberries into the cut-out hole of each brioche bun, then divide the custard mixture equally between the four buns and top each with five more blueberries. Sprinkle over the reserved brioche rubble. Bake in the oven for 20 minutes, or until the custard is just set.

Leave to cool to room temperature, then dust with icing sugar before serving.

Tip These are great warm, but the custard needs time to set so, if you can, resist eating them for at least 20 minutes.

Chorizo and hot smoked fish rice with chorizo oil fried eggs

Serves 4 | Prep 10 minutes | Cook 15 minutes

The Shortcut

Ready-cooked rice pouches are a lifesaver when you're hungry and need to eat as soon as possible. The grains are perfectly cooked and not clumped together and you don't have to worry about preparing, boiling and cooling the rice or ending up with the dready mushy fried rice.

120 g (4 oz) diced chorizo
8 spring onions (scallions), finely chopped white and green parts separated
3 cm (1¼ in) piece of fresh ginger root, peeled and finely chopped
3 garlic cloves, finely chopped
1 red chilli, finely chopped
500 g (1 lb 2 oz/2¾ cups) cooked basmati rice (I used 2 pouches)
5 tablespoons water
2 hot smoked salmon fillets (or smoked mackerel fillets), broken into large flakes
large bunch of coriander (cilantro), leaves picked and stalks roughly chopped
4 eggs

To serve
kimchi
sriracha sauce

I couldn't not include a rice dish for brunch as it is the one meal as a family we all love and I cook it in many different iterations. Here, I've used chorizo as its red spicy oils add so much depth of flavour to the rice and pair so well with the smoked, sweet, delicate flakes of hot smoked salmon.

―――――

Heat a large non-stick frying pan (skillet) over a medium-high heat, add the chorizo and cook for 5 minutes, or until starting to crisp and release its red oils. Push the chorizo to the back side of the pan, then tilt the pan towards you and carefully spoon out most of the hot oil into a small bowl. Set the oil aside.

Add the chopped white spring onions, ginger, garlic, and red chilli to the pan and fry for 2 minutes. Add the cooked rice and stir to coat in the red oils. Add the water and stir-fry for 5 minutes. Add the salmon flakes and fry for 3 minutes, gently stir-frying until everything is piping hot. Fold most of the coriander stalks and leaves through, reserving a few leaves for the top. Divide between four serving bowls.

Return the pan to the heat, turn up the heat to high, add the reserved chorizo oil back to the pan, then, once hot, crack in the eggs and fry to your liking, spooning a little oil over the whites to help them set. Slide on top of the rice and serve with kimchi, sriracha sauce and the reserved coriander.

Tip Use any fish in this dish including prawns (shrimp) and smoked mackerel. I love a fried egg with my spicy rice but if you want to speed this up even further, scramble your eggs into the mixture when you add the rice.

One-pot pasta and noodles

Fail-safe carbonara

Serves 4 | Prep 15 minutes | Cook 20 minutes

The Shortcut

The key to getting this recipe spot on is assembling all your ingredients before you start. Weigh and grate the Parmesan, slice the garlic and have a small heatproof jug nearby to scoop out the pasta water. Dinner will then be ready in next to no time.

olive oil, for drizzling
130 g (4½ oz) diced pancetta
3 garlic cloves, thinly sliced
400 g (14 oz) spaghetti
3 large eggs
salt and freshly ground black
    pepper
125 g (4 oz) finely grated
    Parmesan, plus extra to serve

Tip Don't be tempted to turn up the heat when you add the egg and cheese mixture as a high heat will scramble the eggs. The gentle heat and the residual temperature of the pasta will result in a beautiful silky sauce.

I remember once when I was eight months pregnant, ordering carbonara in my favourite London Italian restaurant. It arrived scrambled. I was utterly indignant and I cried real tears! It was a turning point in my carbonara adventures – I've never ordered one since, but I can say I have happily eaten many using this great fail-safe recipe. The trick is to mix the eggs and Parmesan with the pasta water off the heat so the cheese melts and the mixture is already warm when you add it to the pan and cook it over a very gentle heat.

———

Heat a drizzle of olive oil in a medium saucepan set over a medium-high heat and fry the pancetta for 3 minutes, stirring frequently until starting to take on some colour. Add the garlic and fry for 2 minutes, stirring frequently, until golden and fragrant. Tip the pancetta and garlic into a bowl and set aside.

Put the pan back on the heat, add the spaghetti and enough boiling water to cover. Cook the spaghetti according to the packet instructions, or until it is how you like it.

Meanwhile, in a heatproof bowl, lightly beat the eggs with a fork, removing any gnarly bits. Add plenty of seasoning, then add the cheese and stir to combine.

Scoop out 75 ml (2½ fl oz/5 tablespoons) of hot pasta water, drain the pasta in a colander. Gradually add the reserved water to the egg mixture, stirring constantly until the cheese has melted.

Return the pasta to the pan, turn the heat to its lowest setting and add the egg and cheese mixture, stirring constantly and being very gentle, for 2 minutes, or until the custard is just thickening. Return the garlic, pancetta and any oil collected to the pan and gently stir to combine.

Divide among four plates and serve with extra Parmesan and black pepper.

Creamy garlic mushroom lasagne

Serves 4 | Prep 15 minutes | Cook 40 minutes

The Shortcut

Traditional lasagne involves lots of layering and multiple sauces, but not this one! Breaking up the pasta sheets and submerging them into the creamy mushroom sauce is just the easiest way to make an unctuous, gooey lasagne in a the fraction of the time it would take to make a traditional one.

1 tablespoon olive oil
130 g (4½ oz) bacon lardons
1 onion, chopped
3 garlic cloves, roughly chopped
2 tablespoons thyme leaves
500 g (1 lb 2 oz) chestnut
　　(cremini) mushrooms, sliced
150 g (5 oz) portobello
　　mushrooms, cut into 1 cm
　　(½ in) dice
salt and freshly ground black
　　pepper
1 vegetable stock cube or
　　1 tablespoon miso paste
450 ml (15¼ fl oz/scant 2 cups)
　　boiling water
300 ml (10 fl oz/1¼ cups) double
　　(heavy) cream
grated zest of ½ lemon
handful of flat-leaf parsley,
　　roughly chopped
15 no-precook, dried lasagne
　　sheets, roughly broken
50 g (2 oz) finely grated
　　Parmesan
125 g (4 oz) grated mozzarella
　　and Cheddar mix

Seriously creamy, gooey, rich and comforting lasagne in less than an hour and all made in the one pan? Yes, please! This is by far and away the easiest lasagne recipe I've ever written and one of the most delicious. Leave out the bacon and this would be a great vegetarian main too.

———

Heat the oil in a large, shallow, ovenproof casserole dish (Dutch oven) over a medium-high heat and fry the bacon and onion for 3 minutes, or until they are starting to take on some colour and soften. Add the garlic and thyme and fry for 1 minute.

Add all the mushrooms to the pan with plenty of salt and a good grinding of pepper and fry for 5 minutes, stirring frequently, then cover the pan with a lid and cook for a further 5 minutes.

In a large heatproof bowl or jug, dissolve the stock cube or miso in the boiling water, then stir into the mushrooms. Add the cream, lemon zest and most of the parsley and bring the sauce to the boil.

Gradually add the broken lasagne sheets to the mushroom sauce, pushing the sheets under the surface as you go. Once all of the lasagne has been added, cover with a lid and cook for 15 minutes, stirring every 5 minutes to stop the lasagne sticking together and to re-distribute the mushrooms.

Preheat the grill (broiler) to hot. Sprinkle the Parmesan over the top of the mushrooms and pasta, then cover with the mozzarella and Cheddar mix. Don't worry if some bits of pasta are poking up, as these will become crisp and golden under the grill. Grill (broil) for 3–5 minutes until golden and bubbling, being sure to keep an eye on it so it doesn't burn. Serve immediately, scattered with the reserved parsley.

Tip Frying the mushrooms first gives them some colour and flavour, then covering with a lid lets them release their dark, savoury juices, which form the basis of the sauce.

Chicken cacciatore with orzo

Serves 4 | Prep 10 minutes | Cook 1 hour

The Shortcut

The orzo cooks in the sauce, so there's no separate pan of boiling pasta. You can serve everything from the one dish family-style with a large green salad or some crusty bread and save time at the stove and in the sink.

Chicken cacciatore roughly translates as 'hunter's chicken', and, although I've never hunted anything other than a bargain in my life, I can imagine this would be just the dish to soothe and nourish me if I'd been out hunting. It's a deeply comforting dish that works all year round, warming and cosy on a cold day and bright and easy with a large green salad on a hot day.

———

1 onion, roughly chopped
1 red (bell) pepper, roughly chopped
3 garlic cloves, roughly chopped
3 rosemary sprigs
2 tablespoons olive oil, plus extra for rubbing and drizzling
6 skin-on bone-in chicken thighs
small bunch of flat-leaf parsley, stems chopped and leaves picked
300 g (10½ oz) mixed cherry tomatoes, halved
1 chicken stock cube
400 ml (13 fl oz/generous 1½ cups) boiling water
100 ml (3½ fl oz/scant ½ cup) white wine
100 g (3½ oz/scant 1 cup) mixed stoned (pitted) olives, torn
250 g (9 oz) orzo
salt and freshly ground black pepper

Preheat the oven to 200°C fan (400°F/gas 6).

Put the onion, red pepper, garlic and rosemary into a 30 x 20 x 5 cm (12 x 8 x 2 in) baking tray (pan). Pour over the 2 tablespoons of olive oil, plenty of seasoning and toss to coat everything in the oil. Sit the chicken thighs on top, then rub with oil and season well. Cook in the oven for 30 minutes, shaking the pan halfway through. The chicken should be turning golden and the vegetables becoming tender.

Lift the chicken off the vegetables and transfer to a plate. Add the chopped parsley stems to the tray along with the tomatoes. Sprinkle the stock cube over and pour in the boiling water. Add the wine and olives and give all the ingredients a gentle stir to dissolve the stock cube.

Rinse the orzo in a sieve (fine-mesh strainer) really well, then stir into the tray with some seasoning. Return the chicken to the pan, skin-side up, and cook for 30 minutes, or until the orzo and chicken are cooked through. Scatter with the parsley leaves and drizzle with a little more olive oil before serving.

Tip Rinsing the orzo makes it less starchy so it won't clump together when it's cooking.

Spaghetti with kale, courgette, lemon and ricotta

Serves 4 | Prep 10 minutes | Cook 12–15 minutes

The Shortcut

Throw everything in, stir and about 15 minutes later it's ready to serve. Stirring the pasta makes a lovely silky sauce that clings to the spaghetti.

300 g (10½ oz) spaghetti
2 garlic cloves, finely chopped
grated zest and juice of 2 lemons
¼ teaspoon chilli (hot pepper) flakes, plus extra to serve (if using)
5 tablespoons olive oil, plus extra for drizzling (optional)
salt and freshly ground black pepper
1 litre (34 fl oz/4 cups) boiling water
250 g (9 oz) kale, chopped and any tough stems discarded
100 g (3½ oz) Parmesan, finely grated, plus extra to serve
2 courgettes (zucchini), peeled with a julienne peeler
250 g (9 oz) tub ricotta
handful of crunchy croutons, bashed into rubble (optional)

We eat this dish a lot in our family, especially on days when I want to pack in plenty of greens but not shout about it. The beauty of this dish is that the kale cooks down to a soft, silky addition; its assertiveness tamed by cooking it directly in the pan with the pasta. The lemon zest and juice brighten and the almost raw courgette (zucchini) adds a lovely textural contrast. I love adding a dollop of cold, creamy ricotta on the spaghetti as it adds a welcome richness.

———

In a large, shallow ovenproof casserole dish (Dutch oven) or high-sided frying pan (skillet), add the pasta, garlic, lemon zest, chilli flakes and olive oil. Add plenty of seasoning, then pour in the boiling water and bring to the boil. Drop in the kale, pushing it under the water with a pair of tongs or a long spoon. Cook, stirring the spaghetti and kale frequently for 8–10 minutes, or until the pasta is cooked to your liking. Stir in most of the Parmesan and twirl the pasta to melt.

Drop the courgettes into the pan and let the heat of the pasta wilt the courgette.

In a small bowl, mix the crouton crumbs (if using) with some extra Parmesan and chilli flakes. Divide the pasta between four plates, add a dollop of ricotta and finish with the crunchy crouton crumbs, if you like. I always love a drizzle of extra oil. Just saying!

Tip Add a cup of frozen peas for more greens.

Tomato and mascarpone rigatoni

Serves 4 | Prep 10 minutes | Cook 10–12 minutes

The Shortcut

As the pasta cooks in the sauce, it makes it rich and velvety. This is my favourite way to get a luxurious finish to my pasta sauce without having to introduce lots of extra ingredients or long cooking times.

2 tablespoons olive oil, plus extra
   for drizzling
3 garlic cloves, crushed
½ teaspoon chilli (hot pepper)
   flakes
6 tablespoons tomato purée (paste)
1 teaspoon dried oregano
400 g (14 oz) dried rigatoni or
   penne
700 ml (24 fl oz) bottle good-
   quality passata (sieved tomatoes)
75 g (2½ oz) finely grated
   Parmesan, plus extra to serve
125 g (4 oz) mascarpone
50 ml (1¾ fl oz/3 tablespoons)
   vodka (optional)
salt and freshly ground black
   pepper
handful of basil, torn (optional),
   to serve

There's something so magical that happens when you cook pasta directly in the pan with the ingredients that will form the sauce. The starch from the pasta helps to thicken and velvetise the sauce, resulting in a rich, luxurious texture that belies the simplicity of the ingredients. I love adding a splash of vodka to the sauce as it adds an interesting flavour and elevates the dish to something special. Serve under a blanket of Parmesan for best results.

———

Fill the kettle with water and bring to the boil. Heat the 2 tablespoons of oil in a large, shallow frying pan (skillet) or casserole dish (Dutch oven) set over a medium heat. Add the garlic and chilli flakes and fry for 1 minute, or until fragrant. Add the tomato purée, oregano and pasta. Pour in the passata, then carefully fill the bottle with hot water from the kettle. Swirl to clean out the bottle and add to the pan (I use a dish towel to pick up the bottle). Stir everything together, add plenty of seasoning, then bring to the boil and cook for 8–10 minutes, stirring frequently to stop the pasta sticking to the pan. The pasta should be cooked but still have a little bite.

Add the Parmesan, mascarpone and vodka (if using) to the pasta stir to melt. You might need to add a splash more hot water if the sauce is looking too thick. Taste for seasoning. Ladle into bowls and serve with a drizzle of oil, extra Parmesan and some torn basil, if you like.

Tip Use passata (sieved tomatoes) as they give the sauce a beautiful smooth texture that works so well with the creamy mascarpone.

Spiced squash and gnocchi traybake

Serves 4 | Prep 10 minutes | Cook 1 hour

The Shortcut

I use pre-cut squash as it's so convenient and much quicker than handling an unruly squash. It also works for me as I can use a whole bag for this recipe rather than having half a squash wilting in the refrigerator.

350 g (12 oz) chopped butternut squash
1 onion, chopped
2 tablespoons olive oil
2 garlic cloves, chopped
½–1 teaspoon chilli (hot pepper) flakes (depending on how spicy you like it)
1 tablespoon chopped thyme leaves, plus extra to serve
salt and freshly ground black pepper
2 tablespoons maple syrup
500 g (1 lb 2 oz) fresh gnocchi (from the chiller section)
150 g (5 oz) blue cheese
50 g (2 oz/⅓ cup) pumpkin seeds

This is one of those deeply comforting dishes that you set out not thinking you'll finish then realise you could eat the whole lot on your own. The gnocchi are so soft and pillowy and the blue cheese complements the sweet squash so well. The pumpkin seeds also add a little bit of crunch to contrast with all that soft comfort.

———

Preheat oven to 180°C fan (350°F/gas 4).

Tip the squash and onion into a 30 x 20 x 5 cm (12 x 8 x 2 in) baking tray (pan) and drizzle over the olive oil. Add the garlic, chilli flakes and thyme with plenty of seasoning and toss everything together. Cook in the oven for 30 minutes, shaking the pan halfway through.

Remove the vegetables from the oven and add the maple syrup and gnocchi, stir, then return to the oven and cook for a further 20 minutes.

Dot the blue cheese over the top of the gnocchi and sprinkle with pumpkin seeds. Return to the oven for 5 minutes, or until the cheese is starting to melt and the seeds are toasted. Serve, scattered with extra thyme.

Miso aubergine and noodles

Serves 2 with leftovers | Prep 15 minutes | Cook 30 minutes

The Shortcut

I love ready-cooked noodles, as all it takes to bring them back to life and ready to eat is a short spell in a hot water bath. Drained and tossed through the soft aubergines (eggplants) and sticky sauce they're absolutely delicious. Heating the oil in the tray (pan) before adding the aubergines ensure that they start cooking as soon as they hit the pan.

3 tablespoons lightly flavoured oil
2 aubergines (eggplants), quartered lengthways and cut into 2 cm (¾ in) dice
2 garlic cloves, finely chopped
3 cm (1¼ in) piece of fresh ginger root, peeled and finely chopped
1 tablespoon toasted sesame oil
2 tablespoons miso paste
2 tablespoons maple syrup
2 tablespoons soy sauce
75 ml (2½ fl oz/5 tablespoons) boiling water
300 g (10½ oz) ready-to-eat udon noodles
2 spring onions (scallions), finely chopped, for sprinkling
sesame seeds, for sprinkling
chilli oil (optional), to serve

Aubergine (eggplant) cooked properly is so unctuous and satisfying, teamed with slurpy udon noodles it's just the perfect quick-fix meal. I use the ready-to-eat udon that I just refresh with boiling water, as I find this stops them from breaking up. It also means they're hot when you add them to the aubergine, so they don't need to be cooked any further.

———

Preheat the oven to 200°C fan (400°F/gas 6).

Pour 2 tablespoons of oil into a 30 x 20 x 5 cm (12 x 8 x 2 in) baking tray (pan) and heat in the oven for 3 minutes, or until hot.

Carefully add the aubergine to the hot oil, stir to coat, then drizzle with the remaining oil. The hot oil from the bottom will have been soaked up by the aubergines as they touched the tray. Cook in the oven for 20 minutes, stirring halfway through.

In a large bowl, stir the garlic, ginger, sesame oil, miso, maple syrup, soy sauce and the boiling water together. Pour over the aubergines, stir to coat and cook for a further 10 minutes.

Meanwhile, using the same large bowl (you don't need to wash it), drop in the udon noodles and cover with boiling water. Leave to stand for 2–3 minutes, then use a fork to gently separate the noodles. Drain very well.

Remove the aubergines from the oven, add the udon and gently toss together until the noodles are coated in the syrupy sauce. Sprinkle over the spring onions and sesame seeds and serve with chilli oil, if you like.

'Nduja, prawns and cherry tomatoes

Serves 4 | Prep 10 minutes | Cook 20–25 minutes

The Shortcut

While the 'nduja melts the cherry tomatoes burst and, along with the pasta water, make the most amazing sauce in such a short amount of time. Adding some butter helps to bring all the ingredients together. I use cooked prawns (shrimp) as they heat through in moments.

oilve oil, for drizzling
100 g (3½ oz) 'nduja
1 ciabatta roll, torn into bite-size pieces
2 garlic cloves, finely chopped
400 g (14 oz) short pasta (I used casarecce)
200 g (7 oz) cherry tomatoes, halved
salt and freshly ground black pepper
1 litre (34 fl oz/4 cups) boiling water
25 g (1 oz) butter
180 g (6 oz) cooked large peeled prawns (shrimp)
large handful of flat-leaf parsley, finely chopped

'Nduja is a soft, fiery spreadable salami. It is smoky and spicy and dissolves into the most wonderful pasta sauce with very little input from the cook, while tasting like you've been layering up the seasoning for days. It's my absolute favourite kind of ingredient to have in the refrigerator.

––––––

Heat a drizzle of olive oil in a large, shallow casserole dish (Dutch oven) or high-sided frying pan (skillet) over a medium-high heat. Add the 'nduja and fry for 2–3 minutes until the red oils are starting to flow. Push the 'nduja to one side, add the ciabatta pieces and fry for 5 minutes, or until crisp and stained red from the oils. Remove the ciabatta chunks with a slotted spoon and set aside.

Redistribute the 'nduja in the pan, add the garlic and fry for 1 minute until fragrant.

Add the pasta, cherry tomatoes and plenty of seasoning. Pour in the boiling water and bring to the boil. Cook the pasta stirring every couple of minutes until it is cooked to your liking, about 10–12 minutes. Drop the butter into the pan and shake to melt, then stir in the prawns and allow them to heat through.

Remove the pan from the heat, add the parsley, taste for seasoning and serve immediately scattered with the reserved spicy 'nduja crumbs.

Fried gnocchi puttanesca

Serves 4 or 2 with leftovers | **Prep 5 minutes** | **Cook 15 minutes**

The Shortcut

Shop-bought gnocchi doesn't need any preboiling. Just throwing it in a hot pan with some butter and oil is all it needs.

6 anchovy fillets in olive oil
25 g (1 oz) butter
500 g (1 lb 2 oz) packet fresh gnocchi (from the chiller section)
olive oil, for drizzling
200 g (7 oz) cherry tomatoes on the vine, halved
2 garlic cloves, finely chopped
20 kalamata olives, torn in half
2 tablespoons small capers
large handful of basil, torn, or flat-leaf parsley, roughly chopped

I was late to the gnocchi fan club, but I'm a fully paid-up member now. If you haven't tried them fried then you must. Crunchy on the outside, soft and deeply comforting in the middle. My puttanesca-style fried gnocchi is bright and as easy to eat as it is to make. Juicy, sweet tomatoes, salty olives and capers and melted buttery anchovies work so well with the crunchy, squishy gnocchi.

———

Snip the anchovy fillets into small pieces and add to a large frying pan (skillet) set over a medium-high heat. Add a glug of the oil from the anchovies and the butter and once the butter is bubbling and the anchovies have started to break down add the gnocchi in a single layer. Fry without moving them for 1–2 minutes until golden brown and crisp. Flip the gnocchi over and fry the other sides until golden, then stir the gnocchi around to cook the sides.

Push the gnocchi to one side of the pan, add a drizzle of olive oil and throw in the tomatoes and garlic. Fry for 1–2 minutes until the garlic is fragrant and the tomatoes are starting to soften.

Add the olives and capers to the pan and toss everything together to heat through. Divide between plates and scatter with torn basil or roughly chopped parsley.

Tip I always have a stash of gnocchi in the refrigerator as they're great fried until crisp and served with a fried egg for breakfast or dinner.

Crunchy, soft and saucy chicken cashew nut noodles

Serves 2 | Prep 15 minutes, plus marinating | Cook 28 minutes

The Shortcut

Using a big tray (pan) gives the chicken and vegetables plenty of space to caramelise as they cook and develop great flavour. Cooking ready-to-eat noodles like this is great as some soak up the sauce while the ones sticking up at the top become crispy.

3 cm (1¼ in) piece of fresh ginger root, peeled and grated
2 garlic cloves, grated
4 tablespoons soy sauce
2 tablespoons rice wine vinegar
2 tablespoons runny honey
2 teaspoons toasted sesame oil
4 skinless, boneless chicken thighs, cut into bite-size pieces
50 g (2 oz/⅓ cup) cashews
200 g (7 oz) prepared mixed vegetables (broccoli, baby corn, sugar snap peas)
1 carrot, peeled and thinly sliced on the diagonal
4 spring onions (scallions), 3 cut into 3 cm (1¼ in) pieces, 1 shredded
275 g (10 oz) ready-to-eat egg noodles

To serve (optional)
handful of coriander (cilantro)
chilli oil

This recipe is influenced by Hetty McKinnon's sheet pan chow mein, from her book *To Asia, With Love*. It sounded so delicious I just had to try it. This is my favourite incarnation that I have made, but I haven't encountered a version I haven't loved yet. This is the perfect recipe for using up half packets of vegetables and is an excellent vehicle for any meat or fish. The sauce also works a treat on chicken, steak, salmon and tofu.

———

Mix the ginger, garlic, soy sauce, vinegar, honey and sesame oil together in a large bowl. Add the chopped chicken and leave to stand for 20 minutes, or cover and chill in the refrigerator for up to 24 hours.

Preheat the oven to 180°C fan (350°F/gas 4).

Spread the cashews out on a large, low-sided baking tray (pan), about 39 x 27 x 2 cm (15½ x 10¾ x ¾ in), and toast in the oven for 5–8 minutes, or until golden and fragrant. Remove the nuts from the tray and set aside, then return the tray to the oven to heat up.

Meanwhile, put the mixed vegetables into a colander, pour over a kettle of boiling water and drain very well.

Remove the hot tray from the oven, lift the chicken from the marinade with tongs, shaking off any excess marinade and put the chicken on to the hot tray. Reserve the remaining marinade in the bowl. Add the drained vegetables, sliced carrot and bite-size pieces of spring onion and spread everything out into a single layer. Cook in the oven for 10 minutes.

Remove the tray from the oven, add the noodles and toss everything together. Pour the reserved marinade over the noodles, then return to the oven and cook for a further 10 minutes until the chicken is cooked through.

Serve immediately scattered with the reserved cashews, the coriander and chilli oil, if you like.

Tip If you only have dried egg noodles, put them into a heatproof bowl and cover with boiling water. Leave to stand for 5–10 minutes until soft. Drain very well and pat dry with paper towels before adding to the tray.

Roasted vegetable, pesto and ricotta loaf pan lasagne

Serves 2 | Prep 20 minutes | Cook 45 minutes

The Shortcut

I use shop-bought frozen chargrilled vegetables as they're tasty and somebody else stood at the griddle achieving that tantalising smoky charred flavour so you don't have to. I love a cheesy sauce layer and I don't want to forgo that, so I make this one by combining ricotta, double (heavy) cream and two types of cheese – it's deliciously creamy and gooey.

olive oil, for greasing
250 g (9 oz) frozen, chargrilled vegetables, defrosted
1 garlic clove, grated
400 g (14 oz) tin green lentils, drained
350 g (12 oz) jar tomato pasta sauce
2 tablespoons pesto
3–6 lasagne sheets
salt and freshly ground black pepper
large green salad, to serve

For the ricotta cheese layer
250 g (9 oz) ricotta
75 ml (2½ fl oz/5 tablespoons) double (heavy) cream
50 g (2 oz) Parmesan, finely grated
75 g (2½ oz) grated mozzarella

I love my loaf pan and use it when I need to make something special but want to cut down on the serving size. You'll be thrilled to see that a lasagne sheet fits very well into a loaf pan with minimal trimming. This recipe will yield enough for two hungry people, and is great if you don't want to spend a lot of time making sauces, etc. – just a combination of some simple ingredients and a short spell in the oven.

———

Preheat the oven to 180°C fan (350°F/gas 4) and grease and line a 900 g (2 lb) loaf pan with a long strip of baking parchment. Set aside.

Pat the chargrilled vegetables with paper towels to remove any excess water, then tip into a large bowl with the garlic, lentils, tomato sauce, pesto and plenty of seasoning and gently stir to combine.

For the ricotta cheese layer, in a large bowl, mix together the ricotta, cream, most of the Parmesan and most of the mozzarella. Season very well.

Spoon about one-quarter of the vegetable mixture into the prepared loaf pan, add a layer of ricotta cheese sauce, then top with lasagne sheets to cover all the sauce (one whole sheet, plus one-quarter of a second, broken to fit). Repeat the layering until you have used all the ingredients finishing with a layer of vegetable mixture followed by cheese sauce. Sprinkle the reserved mozzarella and Parmesan over the top.

Cook in the oven for 40–45 minutes until golden and bubbling and the pasta is tender when tested with a knife. Slice and serve with a large green salad.

Easy peasy spaghetti Bolognese

Serves 4–6 | Prep 15 minutes | Cook 30 minutes

The Shortcut

Grating the vegetables straight into the pan not only speeds up the cooking time, the vegetables all cook at the same time. Many Bolognese recipes call for a mix of minced (ground) beef and pork, so I add a couple of good-quality sausages – the fatty meat adds to the richness and the sausage doesn't need long to cook when mixed with the beef. It's a great combination in terms of flavour and texture.

1 tablespoon olive oil
3 good-quality sausages
 (I use Italian-style pork)
1 onion
1 carrot
1 celery stalk
250 g (9 oz) 20% minced
 (ground) beef
4 garlic cloves, grated
1 teaspoon dried oregano
2 bay leaves, dried or fresh
 whatever you have
2 x 400 g (14 oz) tins finely
 chopped tomatoes
1 beef stock cube
200 ml (7 fl oz/scant 1 cup) red
 wine (or use water)
1 tablespoon Worcestershire
 sauce (if you have some)
handful of basil, torn (optional)
100 ml (3½ fl oz/scant ½ cup)
 double (heavy) cream
400 g (14 oz) spaghetti
salt and freshly ground black
 pepper
grated Parmesan, to serve

I didn't grow up eating delicious Bolognese but I have always craved that feeling so many get when they think about their family meals when eating this classic dish. Rich, comforting and bursting with flavour, I want that in my food and this recipe gives me all those feelings as an adult.

———

Heat the olive oil in a large, ovenproof casserole dish (Dutch oven) over a medium-high heat. Push the sausages out of their skins into the hot pan, then coarsely grate the onion on top followed by the carrot and celery, discarding any stringy bits as you go. Fry the sausage and vegetables for 3 minutes, breaking up the sausage with a wooden spoon, until cooked and starting to take on some colour.

Add the beef, increase the heat to high and fry for 3 minutes, stirring frequently to break up the beef until the meat is browned all over. Add the garlic and fry for 1 minute.

Add the oregano, bay leaves and tinned tomatoes. Crumble in the stock cube, then fill one tin with boiled water, swirl it around and pour it into the pan. Add the wine to the other tin and top up with boiled water. Swirl this around and add to the pan. Bring the mixture to the boil, then add the Worcestershire sauce, if using, and cream. Tear in half of the basil (if using) with plenty of seasoning.

Add the spaghetti to the pan, pushing the strands under the sauce, then bring back to the boil and cook for 8–10 minutes, stirring every few minutes, until the pasta is cooked and the sauce is clinging to the strands.

Divide among plates and serve with grated Parmesan and the remaining torn basil.

Salads and vegetables

Shredded chicken salad with spicy peanut dressing

Serves 4 | Prep 20 minutes | Cook 15 minutes

The Shortcut

I just love using rotisserie chicken as part of a recipe, as they're so easy and tasty. If you buy a good-quality bird you can use the carcass to make a quick stock – don't forget to throw in any trimmings from the vegetables into the stock too!

1 rotisserie chicken
100 g (3½ oz) bean sprouts
1 red (bell) pepper, thinly sliced
4 spring onions (scallions), thinly sliced into matchsticks
2 large carrots, thinly sliced into matchsticks (use a julienne peeler if you have one)
½ Chinese leaf lettuce, halved and thinly shredded
30 g (1 oz) bunch of coriander (cilantro)
handful of salted peanuts, roughly chopped

For the dressing

6 tablespoons peanut butter (I use crunchy)
3 tablespoons soy sauce
2 tablespoons maple syrup
1 tablespoon sriracha chilli sauce (if you like a kick)
1 tablespoon rice vinegar
juice of ½ lime, other ½ cut into wedges to serve

This is one of our all-time favourite salads – influenced by gado gado and bang bang chicken salad. We eat it often; I sometimes change the protein and serve juicy prawns (shrimp) instead of chicken, but it also works well with firm smoked tofu or a combination of both if you're trying to cut down on your meat consumption. You can also add any vegetables you want to the salad base, just keep texture in mind when throwing the ingredients into the bowl and you can't go wrong – there are not many things I wouldn't enjoy coated in this spicy peanut dressing!

———

Fill the kettle with water and bring to the boil. Preheat the oven to 200°C fan (400°F/gas 6) and line a 39 x 27 x 2 cm (15½ x 10¾ x ¾ in) baking sheet with baking parchment.

Pull the skin off the chicken and lay in a single layer on the prepared sheet. Cook in the oven for 15 minutes, or until crisp. Leave to cool, then chop or break into shards.

For the dressing, mix all the ingredients together in a bowl. Taste for seasoning and add a little more of any of the ingredients to taste. Set aside.

Put the bean sprouts into a sieve (fine-mesh strainer) or colander, then pour boiling water over the top of them to remove their rawness. Leave to cool.

Pull the meat from the chicken carcass (save this for stock) and pile into your biggest salad bowl. Shred the meat with a couple of forks or with clean hands (you can also do the shredding in the roasting pan now it's cooled), add the vegetables, the bean sprouts and coriander, then pour the dressing over the top and toss to coat. Scatter over the chopped peanuts and crispy chicken skin and serve immediately with lime wedges for squeezing.

Tip This salad can be made in advance and kept chilled, so keep all of the components separate and dress just before serving.

Roasted grape and maple walnut salad

Serves 4 | Prep 10 minutes | Cook 20 minutes

The Shortcut

Roasting grapes changes their flavour from a flat sweetness to sharp, sticky and sweet. They're the perfect partner to walnuts and creamy blue cheese.

300 g (10½ oz) seedless grapes, pulled from the stalks in little bunches (I use a mix of green and red)
3 tablespoons olive oil
1 tablespoon red wine vinegar, plus a splash
salt and freshly ground black pepper
100 g (3½ oz/generous ¾ cup) walnut pieces
2 tablespoons maple syrup
2 heads red chicory (endive), divided into leaves
1 crisp green apple, cored and thinly sliced
2 celery stalks, thinly sliced
1 teaspoon Dijon mustard
150 g (5 oz) soft blue cheese (I used St Agur)
crusty bread, to serve

Roasting grapes brings out their intense sweetness which pairs so well with bitter leaves and blue cheese. This salad is a play on the classic Waldorf salad, which teams fruit, celery and nuts with sharp cheese. My version introduces some beautiful textural contrast from the roasted nuts and juicy grapes. It's always been a classy salad and that I haven't changed.

––––––

Preheat the oven to 180°C fan (350°F/gas 4).

Put the grapes into a 30 x 20 x 5 cm (12 x 8 x 2 in) roasting tin (pan), drizzle over 2 tablespoons of the olive oil and the vinegar, season with salt and pepper and roast in the oven for 10 minutes.

Remove the tin from the oven, add the walnuts and maple syrup and roast for 8–10 minutes until the grapes are tender and the nuts fragrant and toasty. Leave to cool to room temperature.

Lay the chicory on a serving plate, scatter over the thinly sliced apple and celery, then dot the grapes over and scatter the nuts over the salad.

Mix the remaining oil and the mustard into the pan juices with a splash of vinegar and some seasoning, then taste and add more vinegar or oil accordingly. Spoon the dressing over the salad, then dollop the blue cheese on top. Serve immediately with lots of crusty bread.

Tip You can roast the grapes in advance, but keep the nuts separate if you don't plan on serving the salad immediately as they may go soggy.

Easiest chopped salad with ranch dressing

Serves 4–6 | Prep 15 minutes | Cook 25 minutes

The Shortcut

No tiny little diced salad here, just tear, scoop, pile it all on and enjoy!

400 g (14 oz) tin chickpeas
    (garbanzos), drained and rinsed
1 tablespoon olive oil
½ teaspoon smoked paprika
½ teaspoon cumin seeds
flaky sea salt
1 romaine lettuce, torn into
    bite-size pieces
198 g (7 oz) tin sweetcorn, drained
100 g (3½ oz) radishes, scrubbed
3 roasted peppers from a jar,
    roughly torn
4 baby cucumbers, roughly
    chopped
100 g (3½ oz) vine-ripened cherry
    tomatoes
250 g (9 oz) pickled baby beetroot
    (beets), drained
2 avocados, halved and stoned
    (pitted)
100 g (3½ oz) feta

For the dressing
4 tablespoons mayonnaise
6 tablespoons thick Greek-style
    yoghurt
1 teaspoon dried dill
1 teaspoon dried parsley
juice of 1 lemon
½ garlic clove, grated

The idea with a chopped salad is that everything is roughly the same size. Laid out neatly on a plate, it's the ultimate diner-style food and has an air of elegance about it. The different textures and tastes really set this salad apart from more traditional chopped salads. It has everything and leaves you wanting nothing but praise for eating so many delicious vegetables. The creamy, cooling dressing is the perfect foil for the crunchy spiced chickpeas and vegetables.

———

Preheat the oven to 200°C fan (400°F/gas 6).

Throw the chickpeas onto a large roasting tray (pan) and use a piece of paper towel to pat them dry. Drizzle with the olive oil, then sprinkle with the smoked paprika, cumin and plenty of flaky salt. Toss to coat everything in the spices, then roast in the oven for 20–25 minutes, shaking halfway through, until the chickpeas are really crunchy. Leave to cool in the tray.

To assemble the salad, first, make the dressing. Mix the mayonnaise, yoghurt, dried herbs, lemon juice and garlic with plenty of seasoning in a jug. Set aside.

Arrange the lettuce on a platter. Scatter over the sweetcorn, radishes and tear the peppers over the top. Add the baby cucumbers, cherry tomatoes and beetroot. Scoop the avocado from the skin with a spoon, then crumble over the feta and scatter over the crispy chickpeas, pour the dressing all over and serve. Alternatively, push the chickpeas to one sided and layer everything on the roasting tray like the picture.

Tip These chickpeas are so crispy and delicious; they're great served with drinks or as snacks.

All-year-round tomato and mozzarella salad

Serves 4 | Prep 10 minutes | Cook 20 minutes

The Shortcut

A drizzle of oil and salt followed by a short burst in a hot oven can bring an irresistible sweetness and flavour to an otherwise bland tomato.

1 oven-ready precooked ciabatta loaf, torn into bite-size pieces
6 tomatoes, halved
4 tablespoons olive oil, plus extra for drizzling
salt and freshly ground black pepper
200 g (7 oz) mixed colour vine-ripened cherry tomatoes, halved
1 teaspoon caster (superfine) sugar
1–2 teaspoons red wine vinegar
½ garlic clove, grated
2 balls mozzarella, drained and patted dry
large handful of basil

A good tomato can transport me somewhere else, even if it's only in my head. I always keep tomatoes on a windowsill, preferably in the sunshine or in a warmish spot in the kitchen because they keep ripening. A little bit of heat from the oven, a sprinkling of sugar and salt and some good-quality oil can also tease out special flavours so your salad always tastes fresh and intense. This salad is perfect as the crunchy bread soaks up the oil and tomato juices a treat. It's also the best addition to the classic Italian caprese salad trinity of mozzarella, tomato and basil.

———

Preheat the oven to 180°C fan (350°F/gas 4).

Spread the ciabatta pieces out on a large 39 x 27 x 2 cm (15½ x 10¾ x ¾ in) baking tray (pan) with the tomato halves. Drizzle over about 2 tablespoons of olive oil and season with salt and pepper. Cook in the oven for 20 minutes, gently stirring the ciabatta halfway through. Remove from the oven and leave to cool for 10 minutes.

Meanwhile, put the halved cherry tomatoes into a bowl. Sprinkle with plenty of salt and a pinch of sugar and set aside in a warm place for a few minutes.

Remove the cherry tomatoes from the bowl and add to the tray of roasted halves so they get some of the residual heat. Add the vinegar to any juices in the bowl along with the garlic, seasoning and the remaining olive oil. Stir to combine, then pour over the tomatoes and ciabatta.

Tear over the mozzarella and scatter with basil. I serve it on the tray for ease or transfer to a platter. Serve with some extra oil drizzled over the top.

Spiced, roasted cauliflower rice with peas and crispy onions

Serves 4 | Prep 15 minutes, plus soaking | Cook 45 minutes

The Shortcut

Soaking the rice before cooking speeds up the cooking time. If you have never tried roasting cauliflower, it makes such a tasty addition to savoury vegetarian dishes. I just love it.

This is a great dish to have in your repertoire. You can adapt it and change the spiced vegetable base to suit you. If you have impromptu guests, it can be bulked out before serving with a tin of chickpeas, or will sit happily with some grilled (broiled) lamb chops or a spiced roast chicken as a side.

———

400 g (14 oz/2 cups) basmati rice
3 tablespoons lightly flavoured oil
25 g (1 oz) butter
400 g (14 oz) cauliflower florets,
    broken into bite-size pieces
1 onion, cut into wedges through
    the root
2 garlic cloves, finely chopped
2 cm (¾ in) piece of fresh
    ginger root, peeled and finely
    chopped
1½ tablespoons mild curry powder
8 cardamom pods, bashed
1 cinnamon stick
800 ml (27 fl oz/3¼ cups) hot
    vegetable stock
50 g (2 oz) fried onions
small bunch of coriander
    (cilantro), stems finely chopped,
    leaves whole
small bunch of mint, roughly
    chopped
salt and freshly ground black
    pepper
75 g (2½ oz) frozen peas
grated zest and juice of ½ lemon
25 g (1 oz/¼ cup) toasted flaked
    (slivered) almonds
plain yoghurt, to serve

Preheat the oven to 180°C fan (350°F/gas 4).

Rinse the rice in a sieve under cold running water until the water runs clear. Leave to soak in a bowl of warm water for 15 minutes.

Heat 2 tablespoons of the olive oil and the butter in a 30 x 20 x 5 cm (12 x 8 x 2 in) roasting tin (pan) or round 31 cm (12½ in) ceramic dish in the oven for 3 minutes. Carefully add the cauliflower to the tray with the onion, garlic and ginger, then pour over the remaining oilve oil. Sprinkle over the curry powder and nestle the cardamom pods and cinnamon stick in the tray. Cook in the oven for 20 minutes, or until the cauliflower is starting to soften and taken on some colour.

Drain the rice and add it to the tray, then stir to coat in the spices and cauliflower. Pour in the hot stock, half the fried onions, the coriander stems and half of the mint, then add plenty of seasoning. Cover tightly with foil and cook for a further 20 minutes.

Stir in the peas, adding a splash of hot water if the rice looks dry. Cover again and cook for another 5 minutes. Taste for seasoning, add the lemon zest and juice, scatter over the chopped coriander leaves, the rest of the chopped mint, the remaining crispy onions and the flaked almonds and serve with a dollop of yoghurt.

Tip I use a stock cube mixed with boiling water from the kettle – it's the easiest way to make up stock and saves heating it in a separate pan.

Crispy shredded mushrooms with hoisin sauce

Serves 2–4 | Prep 10 minutes | Cook 20 minutes

The Shortcut

Mushrooms cook in a fraction of the time that duck takes to cook. I bet that this is even quicker than a trip to buy a takeaway (take-out).

3 tablespoons lightly flavoured oil
1 tablespoon toasted sesame oil
600 g (1 lb 5 oz) mixed mushrooms
  (I used shiitake, king oyster and oyster)
1½ teaspoons Chinese five spice
3 garlic cloves, finely chopped
3 cm (1¼ in) piece of fresh ginger root, peeled and shredded
2 tablespoons runny honey
2 tablespoons soy sauce

To serve
10 Chinese-style pancakes
½ cucumber, cut into long matchsticks
4 spring onions (scallions), cut into long matchsticks
hoisin sauce

If you like crispy duck from Chinese restaurants then you have to try these crispy mushrooms with Chinese five spice, garlic, ginger and honey. They are addictive. Shredding the mushrooms (which I do with my hands) ensures that some parts get dehydrated and crisp up, other bits get chewy and gnarly and some bits stay plump and juicy… just like roast duck. I've tried to make crispy duck at home, and it's not easy, but these mushrooms are super simple if the craving for something crispy wrapped in a pancake with plum sauce and shredded cucumber and spring onion (scallion) gets the better of you. You can find the thin pancakes in the chiller section of large supermarkets or in Asian stores.

_____

Preheat oven to 200°C fan (400°F/gas 6).

Pour both oils and into a large 39 x 27 x 2 cm (15½ x 10¾ x ¾ in) baking tray (pan) and heat in the oven for 3 minutes until hot.

Shred the mushrooms into thin pieces, about 5 mm (¼ in) thick with your fingertips. Carefully add to the tray and sprinkle over the Chinese five spice. Cook in the oven for 15 minutes.

Stir the garlic, ginger, honey and soy sauce into the mushrooms, then return to the oven and cook for 5 minutes.

Meanwhile, heat the pancakes according to the packet instructions. Bring the pancakes to the table with the mushrooms, cucumber, spring onions and hoisin sauce. Spread some of the sauce onto a pancake, pile with mushrooms and vegetables, roll up and eat immediately.

Tip If you can't find Chinese-style pancakes, soft flour tortillas would work too.

Balsamic onion tart Tatin

Serves 4 | Prep 20 minutes | Cook 40 minutes

The Shortcut

The easiest and quickest way to peel shallots is to soak them in hot water for 10 minutes, as their papery skins just slip off after a hot bath. I am never without a roll of puff pastry (and shortcrust) as my life is often too hectic to take the time to make pastry from scratch.

25 g (1 oz) butter
2 tablespoons olive oil, plus extra for drizzling
400 g (14 oz) shallots, peeled and halved
6 balsamic pickled onions, halved, plus 1 tablespoon of the pickling vinegar
2 tablespoons thyme leaves
3 tablespoons light soft brown sugar
1 tablespoon good-quality aged balsamic vinegar, plus extra for drizzling
320 g (11 oz) packet ready-rolled puff pastry
100 g (3½ oz) soft goat's cheese
handful of roasted chopped walnuts
handful of rocket (arugula)

Some dishes are perfect all year round, whether packed up in a summer picnic or served with a big bowl of creamy mashed potato. I'm pleased to report that this is one of those hardworking dishes that's down to earth for an everyday meal but beautiful enough to make when you're showing off. The trick here is to use a shop-bought pickled onions in balsamic vinegar; they bring a sharpness and sweetness to the tart and brighten up the sweet, sticky shallots they are nestled up with under their blanket of puff pastry. You can serve with dollops of cool, soft goat's cheese and sprinkled with walnuts and some rocket (arugula) dressed with oil and balsamic vinegar, but it's also great as it is.

———

Preheat the oven to 200°C fan (400°F/gas 6).

Add the butter and olive oil to a 30 x 20 x 5 cm (12 x 8 x 2 in) baking tray (pan) and heat in the oven for 3 minutes, or until the butter is melted.

Carefully arrange the shallots and balsamic onion halves in a single layer, cut-side down, in the hot tray. Sprinkle with thyme leaves and roast in the oven for 15 minutes.

Meanwhile, mix the sugar, balsamic vinegar and pickling vinegar together in a bowl, stirring until the sugar dissolves.

Remove the onions from the oven, pour over the sugar mixture, gently lifting the shallots and pickled onions up so that the mixture falls underneath them. I use a butter knife to do this, but a gentle shake of the tray can also work.

Unroll the puff pastry and lay it on top of the shallots and onions. Trim off any excess, then tuck the edges down around the onions and bake for 25 minutes, or until the pastry is golden and puffed up.

To turn the tart out, lay a board or tray bigger than the cooking tray over the top, then carefully and quickly flip the whole thing over so the tart Tatin falls onto the new tray. Dollop over the soft goat's cheese, sprinkle with walnuts and pile on the rocket. Drizzle with a little olive oil and balsamic vinegar over the top, then cut into quarters and serve.

Spicy rice noodle and cucumber salad

Serves 2 | Prep 10 minutes | No cook

The Shortcut

Rice noodles are a shortcut dream as you don't have to cook them, just a quick soak in hot water and they are ready to go. They're also an excellent vehicle for strong flavours as they don't have much flavour of their own.

2 nests vermicelli rice noodles (about 100 g/3½ oz dried weight)
3 teaspoons chilli crisp oil (I like Chiu Chow), plus extra to serve (optional)
1 tablespoon toasted sesame oil
1 tablespoon soy sauce
1 tablespoon rice wine vinegar
1 tablespoon rice wine or dry sherry such as fino
½ teaspoon caster (superfine) sugar
2 spring onions (scallions), finely chopped
½ cucumber, roughly chopped
handful of salted peanuts, roughly chopped

I ate biang biang-style hand-pulled noodles as a takeaway (take-out) so often that I developed an addiction to them. They are so delicious, soft, chewy, spicy and very satisfying. I had to devise my own version as it was becoming an expensive habit, so here you are. This recipe is enough for two but can be very easily doubled. The rice noodles are quick, but for a more authentic take on the hand-pulled noodles use fresh lasagne sheets cut into thick strips and boiled in a saucepan of water with a little bicarbonate of soda (baking soda) – this gives them a little chew.

———

Soak the noodles in a large heatproof bowl of boiling water for 10 minutes, or until soft.

Meanwhile, in a serving bowl, mix together the remaining ingredients, except the peanuts. Stir and taste for seasoning, adding more sugar, vinegar, soy and salt to adjust the flavours to taste. Drain the noodles and add to the bowl. Toss to combine, then leave to stand for 5 minutes before serving with chopped peanuts and extra chilli sauce, if you like.

Thai-style creamy red curry

Serves 4 | Prep 20 minutes | Cook 40 minutes

The Shortcut

I do love a fast furious wok cooking session but I'm not a clean cook and this method helps me to get a great tasting Thai-style curry on the table with minimal effort and minimal cleaning up afterwards – always something to thank yourself for!

3 tablespoons lightly flavoured oil
2 aubergines (eggplants), quartered lengthways and cut into finger-size pieces
1 onion, cut into 2 cm (¾ in) chunks
salt and freshly ground black pepper
3 garlic cloves, grated
3 cm (1¼ in) piece of fresh ginger root, peeled and grated
2–3 tablespoons Thai-style red curry paste (more or less depending on how spicy you like it)
400 ml (13 fl oz) tin coconut milk
1 red (bell) pepper, cut into thick slices
130 g (4½ oz) packet baby corn, halved lengthways
150 g (5 oz) packet sugar snap peas
1–2 tablespoons fish sauce
1 teaspoon light soft brown sugar
juice of ½ lime and other ½ cut into wedges, to serve
handful of coriander (cilantro)
handful of Thai basil
1 red chilli, sliced (optional)
cooked rice or noodles, to serve

The beauty of cooking a Thai-style curry in the oven is that you can get the aubergine (eggplant) very tender and soft, which is something not easily achieved in a saucepan. You can also add anything you want to the base, from chicken to tofu, and as for vegetables, it's perfect for all your favourites – as a rule of thumb, anything that's better crisp, leave until the last 10 minutes to add while everything else can go in at the start. I serve this curry with cooked rice, but noodles would also work wonderfully.

————

Preheat the oven to 200°C fan (400°F/gas 6).

Pour the oil into a 30 x 20 x 5 cm (12 x 8 x 2 in) baking tray (pan) and heat in the oven for 3–5 minutes until really hot.

Carefully add the aubergines and onion to the tray, stir to coat, season, then cook in the oven for 20 minutes, stirring halfway through.

Add the garlic, ginger and curry paste to the tray, stir to coat, then return to the oven and cook for a further 5 minutes.

Stir in the coconut milk, vegetables, fish sauce and sugar. Return to the oven for a further 10 minutes.

Add the lime juice and taste for seasoning, adding a little more lime for sour, sugar for sweetness or fish sauce for sour. Scatter over the coriander, Thai basil and chilli (if using) and serve with rice or noodles and lime wedges.

Tuna and white bean salad

Serves 2 | Prep 5 minutes | No cook

The Shortcut

I use a knife to halve the lemon and slice the onion but that's where I stop with the kitchen equipment. I simply drain everything and add to a large bowl. If I'm sharing, I put it straight onto serving plates, but that just makes a simple recipe even easier!

½ red onion, cut into half moons
juice of ½ lemon (if you have it)
    or 1 tablespoon red or white
    wine vinegar
salt and freshly ground black
    pepper
400 g (14 oz) tin white beans,
    drained
110 g (3½ oz) tin tuna in oil, some
    of the oil reserved for drizzling
1 roasted red (bell) pepper from a
    jar, drained and torn into strips
1 tablespoon capers
handful of black olives, whole or
    roughly chopped
handful of rocket (arugula)

I love a recipe that relies on store cupboard ingredients especially when it tastes this good. This is my ultimate working from home lunch, but I also love it in a buffet. Leave the rocket (arugula) out and the bean and tuna base will be good in the refrigerator for a couple of days; just refresh with a drizzle of oil before serving. For a stylish lunch for friends, just pile on top of good-quality toasted sourdough and, voilà, it's ready.

———

Add the onion to a bowl and pour over the lemon juice or vinegar. Season with plenty of salt and leave to stand for a few minutes.

Add the beans to the onions followed by the tuna, torn pepper, capers, olives and a drizzle of oil from the tuna. Taste for seasoning, add the rocket, then toss to combine. Serve immediately.

Tip You can swap the ingredients for similar ones, such as using chickpeas (garbanzos) instead of the white beans, spring onions (scallions) instead of the onion, green olives instead of black and sardines for the tuna... you get the picture. It works.

A family falafel with tahini yoghurt

Serves 4 | Prep 15 minutes | Cook 30 minutes

The Shortcut

Sometimes it's too much effort to stand and make balls of falafels, so this dish is for those times, as you simply put the falafel mix in a hot tray (pan). Gently turning the mixture during cooking provides that characteristic falafel ball crunch without the hard labour of rolling the mix into balls and deep-frying.

This dish is such a hit in our family, as it's delicious to eat and so easy to prepare. Getting the pan nice and hot creates a crunchy base layer, which is then gently exposed during cooking to crisp up even more. So much quicker and easier than shaping and deep-frying falafel balls but equally flavoursome. If we're trying to reduce our bread intake, we have this mix on top of a large chopped salad. The tahini yoghurt is the stuff of dreams and also works very well as a dip for crisped pittas and crunchy veg.

———

2 x 400 g (14 oz) tins chickpeas (garbanzos), drained
salt
3 garlic cloves, roughly chopped
1 onion, roughly chopped
1 teaspoon ground coriander
1 teaspoon sumac, plus extra to serve
1 teaspoon paprika
1 tablespoon cornflour (cornstarch)
handful of flat-leaf parsley, roughly chopped
handful of coriander (cilantro), roughly chopped
3 tablespoons olive oil, plus extra for drizzling
2 teaspoons cumin seeds

For the garlic tahini sauce
100 g (3½ oz) Greek-style yoghurt
2 tablespoons tahini
1 garlic clove, grated

To serve
pitta bread or wraps
zoug or hot sauce or both
chopped cucumber, lettuce and tomato
pickles
½ red onion, sliced

Preheat the oven to 200°C fan (400°F/gas 6).

Pulse the chickpeas, 1 teaspoon of salt, chopped garlic, onion, ground coriander, sumac and paprika three to four times in a food processor until everything is combined and the chickpeas are mostly broken down, but with some remaining whole. Add the cornflour, chopped herbs and pulse once more to incorporate them. Set aside.

Pour the olive oil into a 30 x 20 x 5 cm (12 x 8 x 2 in) baking tray (pan), add the cumin seeds and heat in the oven for 3 minutes. Carefully spoon the chickpea mixture into the tray, stirring in the cumin seeds as you go. Gently spread out, leaving the surface craggy and uneven. Drizzle a little olive oil over the top and cook for 25 minutes, gently turning the falafel over with a spoon halfway through cooking to create an uneven texture and so the bottom crunchy layer is on top.

Meanwhile, mix together the yoghurt, tahini and garlic with a good pinch of salt in a bowl until smooth. Set aside.

Warm the pittas or wraps in the hot oven, spoon on the falafel and a dollop of tahini yoghurt, add some zoug or hot sauce and salad and eat with pickles and sliced red onion.

Chicken and fish

Chicken fajita-style traybake with avocado salsa

Serves 4 | Prep 20 minutes | Cook 25 minutes

The Shortcut

Throw it all on a tray, put it into the oven and forget about it.

2 skinless, boneless chicken breasts, chopped into bite-size pieces
1 red (bell) pepper, sliced into strips
1 yellow (bell) pepper, sliced into strips
1 onion, ½ cut into thin wedges through the root, ½ finely chopped
2 tablespoons olive oil
salt and freshly ground black pepper
2 teaspoons smoked paprika
2 teaspoons dried oregano
2 teaspoons garlic granules
1 teaspoon ground cumin
400 g (14 oz) tin black beans, drained and rinsed
250 g (9 oz) pouch cooked rice
3 tablespoons water
small bunch of coriander (cilantro), roughly chopped, plus a little extra for the salsa

For the salsa
1 onion, roughly chopped
3 ripe tomatoes, roughly chopped
1 ripe avocado, halved, stoned (pitted) and flesh scooped out
salt and freshly ground black pepper
juice of 1 lime, plus extra lime wedges to serve

To serve
soft tortillas
sour cream
grated Cheddar

My favourite way to eat fajitas is when I'm relaxed and feeling excited about life. I often serve these chicken fajitas for brunch or a casual dinner. They are just so informal, hands on and deliciously messy. I love to serve all the usual accompaniments, including sour cream, soft flour tortillas, salsa and grated cheese alongside the main traybake.

———

Preheat the oven to 180°C fan (350°F/gas 4).

Put the chicken, peppers and onion on to a low-sided 39 x 27 x 2 cm (15½ x 10¾ x ¾ in) baking tray (pan). Drizzle over the olive oil, then sprinkle over the spices and plenty of seasoning. Toss together with your hands until everything is coated in the spices. Cook in the oven for 20 minutes, stirring halfway through. The chicken should be cooked through and the peppers starting to soften and char in places.

Add the black beans to the tray with the cooked rice and water, stir, then return to the oven for 5 minutes to heat through.

To make the salsa, mix the chopped onion, chopped tomatoes, avocado and a little chopped coriander together in a small bowl. Add plenty of seasoning and the lime juice and set aside.

Remove the tray from the oven, scatter over the chopped coriander. Serve with the salsa, soft flour tortillas, a dollop of sour cream, grated Cheddar and lime wedges.

Tip If you have any leftovers, just pop them all onto a large tortilla, then roll up and wrap in foil, burrito-style. This can then be reheated in the foil for 10 minutes in a hot oven for a quick meal.

Chicken, chorizo and potato stew with smoky aioli

Serves 4 | Prep 15 minutes | Cook 55 minutes

The Shortcut

The oil from the chorizo not only flavours the base of the dish, a little is scooped out and used to flavour the aioli too. I love ingredients that work so hard for you.

My favourite meals are those that can take me on holiday without moving from the comfort of my home and this is it. The potatoes, chorizo and chicken are cooked together and crisped up before wine and leeks are added to the tray (pan) – they add a perfect complementary sweetness to this dish.

_____

6 bone-in, skin-on chicken thighs
500 g (1 lb 2 oz) baby new
    potatoes, large ones halved
100 g (3½ oz) chorizo, thinly sliced
2 tablespoons olive oil
salt and freshly ground black
    pepper
200 ml (7 fl oz/scant 1 cup) dry
    white wine
1 chicken stock cube
100 ml (3½ fl oz/scant ½ cup)
    boiling water
1 leek, sliced into 1 cm (½ in) rings
100 g (3½ oz) baby spinach
grated zest of ½ lemon

For the smoky aioli
1 teaspoon smoked paprika
1 garlic clove, crushed or grated
8 tablespoons good-quality
    mayonnaise

Preheat the oven to 200°C fan (400°F/gas 6).

Arrange the chicken, potatoes and chorizo in a 30 x 20 x 5 cm (12 x 8 x 2 in) baking tray (pan), pour over the olive oil and season really well. Toss to coat, then put the chicken skin-side up and cook in the oven for 25 minutes, or until the chicken is turning golden and the chorizo has released some of its lovely red oils.

Meanwhile, in a bowl, mix the wine, stock cube, boiling water and leek together and season very well.

Remove the tray from the oven and carefully spoon out about 2 tablespoons of the red chorizo oil into a small bowl and set aside. Pour the wine mixture into the tray and stir, making sure the chicken is on top. Return to the oven for 30 minutes, or until the chicken is cooked through and the potatoes are very tender.

For the smoky aioli, mix the reserved chorizo oil, the smoked paprika, crushed garlic and mayonnaise with some seasoning together in a small bowl. Set aside.

Put the chicken onto serving plates and toss the spinach through the potatoes, allowing the heat of the tray to wilt the spinach. Scatter over the lemon zest and taste for seasoning. Serve immediately with the chicken and a dollop of smoky aioli.

Tip Buy a decent bottle of dry white wine for this and get it chilled to drink with the meal – it'll be delicious, I promise.

Harissa chicken, courgettes and chickpeas with roasted garlic yoghurt

Serves 4 | Prep 15 minutes | Cook 45 minutes

The Shortcut

Slashing the chicken legs not only helps the flavour of the harissa to penetrate the flesh it also speeds up the cooking time.

2 tablespoons olive oil, plus extra
    for greasing
4 tablespoons harissa paste
4 skin-on, bone-in chicken leg
    portions, scored 2–3 times
4 garlic cloves, skin on and
    left whole
2 courgettes (zucchini), thickly
    sliced on the diagonal
1 lemon, halved
salt and freshly ground black
    pepper
660 g (1 lb 7 oz) jar big chickpeas
    (garbanzos), drained
400 g (14 oz) vine-ripened cherry
    tomatoes, broken into small
    bunches
200 g (7 oz) Greek-style yoghurt
50 g (2 oz) green olives, stoned
    (pitted) and roughly chopped
handful of flat-leaf parsley,
    roughly chopped

I love dinners like this where the oven does all of the work for you and you end up with a meal that not only looks amazing but has so much flavour and texture just by being cooked altogether. Harissa is a wonderful ingredient to have in the refrigerator – a spoonful stirred into a vegetable soup, or a dollop mixed into mayonnaise can transform the mundane into something special.

———

Preheat the oven to 200°C fan (400°F/gas 6) and grease a very large 39 x 27 x 2 cm (15½ x 10¾ x ¾ in) baking tray (pan).

Spread the harissa over the chicken, rubbing it into the scores. Lay the chicken on the prepared tray, add the garlic and courgettes, then squeeze over half of the lemon and add both halves to the tray. Season very well. Drizzle everything with the olive oil, toss to coat, then put in the chicken skin-side up and roast in the oven for 30 minutes.

Remove the tray from the oven, take out the roasted garlic cloves and the unsqueezed lemon from the tray and set aside.

Stir the chickpeas into the tray, add the tomatoes and return to the oven for 15 minutes, or until the chicken is cooked through and golden and the tomatoes are soft.

Meanwhile, push the garlic from its papery skins and mix with the Greek yoghurt in a small bowl. Squeeze in the juice from the roasted lemon, season and set aside.

Remove the tray from the oven, scatter with olives and parsley and serve immediately with the roasted garlic yoghurt.

Tip Jarred chickpeas are so plump and much softer than canned chickpeas and they're definitely worth the slightly higher price for a delicious dish like this, which is all about the textures and robust flavours.

Easy coq au vin

Serves 4 | **Prep 20 minutes** | **Cook 1 hour 20 minutes**

The Shortcut

Aside from standing with your chicken as it browns, you can leave this dish to happily do its thing unattended. I love using pickled onions as you don't have to peel them and they add such a welcome zingy flavour to this rich stew.

12 silverskin pickled onions, halved
2 tablespoons olive oil
4 skin-on, bone-in chicken leg portions
salt and freshly ground black pepper
80 g (3 oz) smoked bacon lardons or pancetta cubes or 3 rashers (slices) bacon, chopped
1 onion, chopped
300 g (10½ oz) chestnut (cremini) mushrooms, quartered
2 garlic cloves, chopped
2 teaspoons plain (all-purpose) flour
2 fresh or dried bay leaves (whatever you have)
small bunch of thyme
4 carrots, cut into chunks
500 ml (17 fl oz/2 cups) red wine
1 chicken stock cube
200 ml (7 fl oz/scant 1 cup) boiling water
mashed potato, to serve

Give anything a French name and it sounds fancy, doesn't it? I love this dish, as it couldn't be simpler. You do have to brown off the chicken legs, but they simply sit in the pan for 10 minutes. You'll notice that once they are beautiful and golden they will self release, which means they won't be stuck to the pan and you won't have a hard time cleaning it later. I add little silverskin pickled onions in place of the more traditional baby onions or shallots, as they're ready peeled and ready to eat, and, although I soak them in boiling water, their residual vinegar just adds a pop of brightness and tang to this traditionally rich dish. Since my last book I haven't embraced mashing potatoes so use shop-bought like me, if you prefer.

_____

Put the pickled onions into a bowl and cover with boiling water. Set aside.

Meanwhile, heat the olive oil in a large, ovenproof casserole dish (Dutch oven) over a medium-high heat. Season the chicken with salt, then place in the pan, skin-side down, and cook for 10 minutes. Move them around a little so they don't burn but leave the skin to crisp.

Flip the chicken over and push to one side of the pan, sitting them up against the edge to make some room. Add the bacon, onion and mushrooms and fry for 5 minutes. Stir in the garlic and fry for a further minute. Stir in the flour and cook for 1 minute.

Drop in the bay leaves, thyme and carrots, then pour in the red wine. Add the stock cube and boiling water, stir, bring to a simmer, season very well, cover and simmer gently for 1 hour.

Drain the pickled onions and add to the pan to heat through. Serve with mashed potato.

Cosy spiced, roast chicken with Middle Eastern-style rice and lentils

Serves 4 | Prep 15 minutes, plus 30 minutes standing | Cook 1 hour, plus 10 minutes standing

The Shortcut

Cut your prep with a pouch of rice and tin of lentils. The oven should be hot when you put the chicken in to cook, as this helps reduce the overall cooking time. Sitting the chicken on top of the onions allows the heat to circulate all around the bird as well as being great for collecting those unctuous pan juices.

1 tablespoon fine sea salt
1 teaspoon ground cinnamon
1 teaspoon ground cumin
1 teaspoon ground coriander
1 teaspoon ground paprika
1 fat garlic clove, grated
1.3 kg (3 lb) whole chicken
1 lemon, halved
2 red onions, cut into wedges
    through the root
1 tablespoon olive oil
25 g (1 oz) soft butter
2 tablespoons pomegranate
    molasses
400 g (14 oz) tin green lentils,
    drained
250 g (9 oz) pouch cooked rice
salt and freshly ground black
    pepper
handful of pomegranate seeds
handful of crispy onions
handful of coriander (cilantro),
    stems finely chopped and leaves
    picked
handful of mint
Greek yoghurt, to serve (optional)

The warming spices, garlic and salt mixture that's rubbed into the chicken's skin at the start acts as a delicious seasoning and also a quick-dry brine, keeping your bird really juicy. I use a tin of lentils and a pouch of rice in this recipe, both readily available, cheap and very convenient – no standing over boiling pans for us!

———

In a bowl, mix the sea salt with the ground spices and garlic to form a grainy paste. Rub the chicken all over inside and out with the paste. Stuff half of the lemon into the bird's cavity, then leave the chicken to stand for 30 minutes at room temperature.

Meanwhile, preheat the oven to 200°C fan (400°F/ gas 6).

Arrange the onions in a layer on the bottom of a 30 x 20 x 5 cm (12 x 8 x 2 in) baking tray (pan). Season well and drizzle over 1 tablespoon of olive oil. Dot the butter over the chicken breast and sit it on top of the onions. Roast in the oven for 30 minutes.

Remove the tray and stir the onions. Reduce the oven temperature to 180°C fan (350°F/gas 4), then return the tray to the oven and roast for a further 25 minutes. Pour the pomegranate molasses over the chicken and cook for 5 minutes, or until sticky.

Lift the chicken onto a board to rest. Stir the lentils and rice into the onions, scraping down the pan to stir in any sticky juices, then return to the oven to warm through while the chicken rests.

Stir the pomegranate seeds and herbs through the rice. Scatter with crispy onions and serve with slices of chicken and a dollop of yoghurt, if you like.

Tip Always keep crispy onions in your store cupboard as they just add to everything you will eat, from fried eggs to instant noodles, making almost everything better.

Creamy coconut chicken curry and rice

Serves 4 with leftovers | Prep 15 minutes, plus standing | Cook 35 minutes

The Shortcut

Rinsing the rice and using curry paste from a jar both help to shorten the cooking time as well as making this a fast and delicious feast.

300 g (10½ oz/1½ cups) basmati rice
2 tablespoons lightly flavoured oil
2 onions, sliced
salt
4 garlic cloves, grated
4 cm (1½ in) piece of fresh ginger root, peeled and grated
1 tablespoon curry powder
3 tablespoons tikka masala paste
8 skinless, boneless chicken thighs, cut into bite-size pieces
400 ml (13 fl oz) tin coconut milk
1 tin finely chopped tomatoes

To serve
handful of coriander (cilantro), chopped
toasted coconut flakes
1 green finger chilli, sliced (optional)
1 lemon, cut into wedges

For those evenings when you just need something so comforting and delicious this dish is it. The rice is tender and creamy, the chicken is soft and spicy and it's all just so easy to eat.

——

Rinse the rice under cold running water until it runs clear, then transfer to a bowl, cover with warm water and leave to stand for 15 minutes.

Heat the oil in a large, shallow, ovenproof casserole dish (Dutch oven) set over a medium-high heat, add the onions and plenty of salt and fry for 8 minutes, or until they are light golden and softened. Add the garlic, ginger and fry for 1 minute, or until fragrant. Add the curry powder, masala paste and chicken and stir-fry for 5 minutes, or until the chicken is sealed and the curry paste is cooked out. Pour in the coconut milk and chopped tomatoes. Half-fill the tomato tin with water, swirl and add to the pan, then bring to a simmer and cook for 5 minutes, stirring occasionally.

Drain the rice really well, sprinkle it into the chicken and submerge the rice under the sauce. Cook for 5 minutes. Reduce the heat to low and cook for a further 8 minutes.

Serve with chopped coriander, toasted coconut and green chilli sprinkled over the top and lemon wedges for squeezing over.

Tip You can make this vegetarian by using button mushrooms instead of the chicken. The texture of the whole button mushrooms works really well with the spices and creamy coconut.

Crispiest spicy chicken wings with cooling slaw

Serves 2–4 | Prep 15 minutes | Cook 45 minutes

The Shortcut

No deep-frying wings in batches, just lay them out on a baking tray (pan) and pop them into the oven. You want a large tray for this so the heat can circulate. I also dust my wings in a strong bag – let's minimise the clean up, people.

1.5 kg (3 lb 5 oz) chicken wings
½ teaspoon baking powder
4 tablespoons plain (all-purpose) flour
¼ teaspoon cayenne pepper
1 teaspoon paprika
1 teaspoon garlic powder
1 teaspoon fine salt
hot sauce, to serve (I like Frank's)

For the slaw
½ white cabbage, finely shredded
4 spring onions (scallions), thinly sliced
2 celery stalks, thinly sliced
1 crisp apple, cored and thinly sliced (I love Granny Smith)
2 tablespoon Greek-style yoghurt
2 tablespoons good-quality mayonnaise
salt and freshly ground black pepper

These chicken wings are tossed in a mix of flour and a little baking powder, which makes them super crispy. You'll think you're eating deep-fried wings when it's the hard work of the oven that you have to thank for that delicious crispy skin. I love a little chilli kick with my wings, but if you don't, then replace the cayenne with paprika.

———

Take the chicken wings out of the refrigerator about 20–30 minutes before you want to start cooking them.

Preheat the oven to 200°C fan (400°F/gas 6) and line a large 37 x 33 x 4 cm (14½ x 13 x 1½ in) baking tray (pan) with baking parchment.

Put the baking powder, flour and spices into a big bag (I usually use an old paper shopper or large ziplock bag). Add the fine salt and shake to combine. Drop the chicken wings into the bag, seal the bag, then shake the bag to coat the wings in the flour.

Remove the wings from the bag, shaking off any excess flour, and arrange in a single layer on the prepared tray. Cook in the oven for 45 minutes, or until the wings are golden brown and crispy.

Meanwhile, for the slaw, mix all the ingredients together in a bowl, season very well, then cover and chill until ready to serve with the chicken wings.

Serve the chicken wings with hot sauce and slaw.

Chicken kebab, salad and chip wraps

Serves 4 | Prep 20 minutes, plus marinating | Cook 30 minutes

The Shortcut

Making one large kebab is so much quicker than threading multiple skewers. It also means that the meat stays tender where it touches. The onions at the ends of the skewers are delicious broken up and added to your kebab with the chicken and chips.

8 skinless, boneless chicken thighs, cut into thirds
2 garlic cloves, grated
grated zest and juice of ½ lemon
1 teaspoon runny honey
100 g (3½ oz) plain yoghurt
1 small red onion, halved
2 long Turkish peppers, halved or 1 green (bell) pepper, cut into 4 pieces
2 tablespoons lightly flavoured oil
500 g (1 lb 2 oz) frozen oven-cook French fries
salt and freshly ground black pepper

For the spice mix
2 teaspoons dried oregano
2 teaspoons sweet smoked paprika
2 teaspoons garlic salt
salt and freshly ground black pepper

For the salad
2 tomatoes, chopped
1 small red onion, sliced
½ cucumber, chopped

To serve
2–4 soft wraps or naan bread (depending on size)
Greek yoghurt
chilli sauce
½ lemon, cut into wedges

Threading the kebabs with onions at each end helps to lift the meat off the tray so the hot air can circulate around the chicken and cook it evenly. Adding a few chips (fries) to a kebab is a real game changer in kebab eating – they add a lovely crunch but also a nice soft texture to soak up any juices. Heaven.

———

For the spice mix, in a small bowl, mix together the dried oregano, paprika, garlic salt and some seasoning. Set aside.

Put the chicken into a large bowl and add half of the spice mix, the garlic, lemon zest and juice, honey and yoghurt. Stir to coat, then cover and leave to marinate for 10 minutes, or up to 24 hours in the refrigerator.

When ready to cook, preheat the oven to 200°C fan (400°F/gas 6) and put a large baking tray (pan) into the oven to heat up (I actually use the oven shelf for this).

Using two large skewers, hold them together so they run parallel to each other, then thread half an onion onto them, followed by the chicken pieces, then add the Turkish pepper along their length in between the chicken and finish with the remaining half of onion. Set aside.

Carefully remove the hot tray, add the oil, then tip the oven chips into it and sprinkle the remaining spice mix all over them, clearing a space down the centre of the tray for the chicken kebabs. Cook in the oven for 25–30 minutes, turning the chips halfway through.

For the salad, mix all the ingredients together in a large bowl with plenty of seasoning. Heat your chosen fluffy wraps in the oven – the best way to do this is to splash them with a little water, then pop into the hot oven for 1–2 minutes.

Spread each wrap with a dollop of cold yoghurt, pile on some salad, then push some of the chicken and peppers on top and a pile of chips. Devour with chilli sauce and a lemon wedge to squeeze over.

No-fuss chicken Kiev with crunchy roast potatoes

Serves 4 | Prep 20 minutes | Cook 1 hour

The Shortcut

Doing the egging and coating in flour in a sandwich bag really saves on washing-up time. And pouring over the all important garlic butter versus stuffing it inside the chicken breasts is literally hours saved in chilling, stuffing, sealing, cleaning up, etc.

2 tablespoons olive oil, plus extra for greasing and drizzling
1 kg (2 lb 4 oz) baby new potatoes
4 skinless, boneless chicken breasts
200 g (7 oz/2 cups) dried breadcrumbs
1 teaspoon paprika
1 teaspoon garlic granules
salt and freshly ground black pepper
3 tablespoons plain (all-purpose) flour
2 eggs, lightly beaten

For the garlic butter
125 g (4 oz) soft butter
3 garlic cloves, crushed or grated
large handful of flat-leaf parsley, finely chopped

Is there a better meal than one smothered liberally in garlic butter? I don't think so. The beauty of this recipe is that the chicken stays tender and juicy coated in its crisp crumb, and the craggy potatoes are the perfect vehicle for eating the delicious garlic butter. I love this served with an old school salad of leaves, tomato, cucumber, tinned sweetcorn and thinly sliced red onion – proper retro!

———

Preheat the oven to 200°C fan (400°F/gas 6) and lightly oil a wire rack and set aside.

Cook the potatoes in a microwave-safe bowl in the microwave on high for 10 minutes, or until starting to soften. Tip the potatoes into a large 39 x 27 x 2 cm (15 x 10¾ x ¾ in) baking tray (pan) and use the tines of a fork or a potato masher to lightly smash them. Drizzle with the olive oil and season very well. Roast in the oven for 10 minutes.

Meanwhile, put the chicken breasts into a strong, large sandwich bag, push the air out, then lay the bag flat and use a rolling pin to flatten the breasts to about 2 cm (¾ in) thick all over. (You might have to do this in batches if you don't have a big bag.)

Mix the breadcrumbs, paprika, garlic granules and plenty of seasoning together in a large bowl and set aside.

Open the bag, leaving the breasts inside, and sprinkle the flour over the top, then turn to coat so they are covered in flour.

With the chicken breasts still in the bag, pour in the beaten eggs and turn to coat. Working quickly, lift the breasts out one at a time and coat in the seasoned breadcrumbs, transferring them to the oiled wire rack as you go.

continued overleaf...

Sit the rack carefully on top of the tray containing the potatoes, drizzle each breast with a little olive oil, then cook in the oven for 35–40 minutes until the chicken is cooked through and the coating is crisp.

For the garlic butter, mix the butter, garlic and parsley together in a small bowl. Remove the tray from the oven and lift the chicken rack off the tray. Stir half the garlic butter into the potatoes to coat, then divide between serving plates. Serve the chicken with a dollop of garlic butter to melt into those crispy crumbs.

Tip There are plenty of ways to vary this recipe. Serve it with aioli or just mayonnaise, or try different herbs in the butter. Why not add a handful of whole garlic cloves in their skins, then squeeze out the garlic as you enjoy your meal.

Fish, chips and tartare peas

Serves 4 | Prep 20 minutes | Cook 40 minutes

The Shortcut

Make sure your oven is hot. Leave the skin on your potatoes as it adds both flavour and texture, gives a lovely crunch and saves time peeling. My method of breadcrumbing also saves on the washing-up and messy hands.

3 tablespoons lightly flavoured oil, rapeseed works well
5 large floury (mealy) potatoes, cut into 1 cm (½ in) chips
4 x 120 g (4 oz) skinless firm white fish fillets (cod, haddock, hake or your favourite)
3 tablespoons plain (all-purpose) flour
salt and freshly ground black pepper
1 large egg, lightly beaten
75 g (2½ oz/1¼ cups) golden breadcrumbs

For the tartare peas
350 g (12 oz/2¼ cups) frozen peas
1 shallot, finely chopped
2 gherkins, finely chopped
1 tablespoon capers, roughly chopped
2 tablespoons mayonnaise
1 teaspoon Dijon mustard
grated zest and juice of ½ lemon

To serve
½ lemon, cut into wedges
buttered bread
ketchup (optional)

I've lost track of how many times I've written this but you won't be surprised to hear that fish and chips are one of my all-time favourite foods. For me, like ice cream or popcorn, fish and chips are happy food. They say Friday night, seaside and a good day out. Being from the north it's easy to find great fish and chips, but I'm yet to find a great chippy near my current home – that's close enough so the chips and fish will still be hot when I get home (I try, I really do!). Now, I like making them myself at home, and they're consistently good and hot! Serve with white bread spread with salty butter and malt vinegar – heaven!

———

Preheat the oven to 220°C fan (425°F/gas 7).

Carefully remove the shelf from your oven or use a large 39 x 27 x 2 cm (15½ x 10¾ x ¾ in) baking tray (pan). Line the shelf or baking tray with baking parchment and drizzle with a little of the oil. Arrange the chips in a single layer, drizzle over the remaining oil and cook in the oven for 25 minutes, flipping the chips halfway through with a spatula.

Meanwhile, put the fish into a strong ziplock bag. Add plenty of seasoning to the flour, then dust all over the fish. Seal the bag and shake to make sure the fish is coated in flour. Lay the bag flat and pour the beaten egg over the floured fish, then gently turn the fish to coat in the egg. Spread the breadcrumbs out on a plate. Lift the fish from the bag and gently drop them into the breadcrumbs, turning them to coat.

Make 4 spaces in the chips for the fish, then return the tray to the oven for 10–15 minutes, depending on the thickness of the fillets, or until the chips are tender and the fish is cooked through.

continued overleaf...

Meanwhile, for the tartare peas, put the peas and shallot into a sieve (fine-mesh strainer) and pour boiled hot water over them. Transfer to a serving bowl and roughly mash the peas with a fork. Add the gherkins, capers, mayonnaise and mustard, stir, then add the lemon zest and juice. Taste for seasoning and add a little more of what you think is needed to balance out the flavours. Set aside.

Serve the fish and chips with some peas, lemon wedges, ketchup (if you like) and plenty of bread and butter. A pot of tea is always a welcome addition too... just saying!

Tip I use the oven tray from inside of the oven as this is big enough to fit the chips and fish and allows room for everything to crisp up nicely. Remove the peas from the freezer before you start cooking so they can begin to defrost in the heat of the kitchen.

Garlic mussels

Serves 2 | Prep 10 minutes | Cook 24 minutes

The Shortcut

Get the oven very hot and the mussels will simply steam open. You don't need to stand and shake the pan, and best of all, the beautiful seafood juices are caught in the tray (pan).

Is there anything better than a generous dish of mussels and a nice little something on the side to dunk into the juices? I don't think so. For me, a large tray of mussels immediately takes me back to my holidays or dining out in restaurants, but they're so simple to make at home, and as we've all learned over the past couple of years, sometimes you have to holiday at home!

25 g (1 oz) butter
1 tablespoon olive oil
2 shallots or ½ onion, finely chopped
2 garlic cloves, finely chopped
100 ml (3½ fl oz/scant ½ cup) dry white wine
1 kg (2 lb 4 oz) live mussels, scrubbed clean and beards removed (discard any mussels that are open)
salt and freshly ground black pepper
50 ml (1¾ fl oz/3 tablespoons) double (heavy) cream
large handful of flat-leaf parsley, chopped

To serve

chips to serve, oven chips or from the chip shop (your choice)
crusty bread, for dunking and mopping up the juices

Preheat the oven to 200°C fan (400°F/gas 6).

Heat the butter and oil in a 30 x 20 x 5 cm (12 x 8 x 2 in) baking tray (pan) in the oven for 2 minutes, or until the butter has melted. Stir in the shallots and garlic and cook in the oven for 2 minutes.

Stir the shallots, then pour in the white wine, add the mussels and some seasoning. Shake the pan, cover with foil and cook for 20 minutes.

Pour the cream into the tray, add the chopped parsley and stir to coat the mussels with all the delicious juices. Discard any mussels that haven't opened. Serve with chips and/or crusty bread.

Tip If you're serving oven French fries, slip them into the oven from frozen 5 minutes before you put the mussels in to cook and they'll be ready together.

Toasty coconut rice with salmon

Serves 4 | **Prep 5 minutes, plus soaking and standing** | **Cook 15 minutes**

The Shortcuts

The rice is cooked in creamy coconut milk and the salmon is steamed directly on top of the rice, making it both quick and easy. Then there's more coconut to reallly intensify the flavour perfectly through the dish. It's a great ingredient to have to hand. Soaking the rice before cooking cuts the cook time right down so dinner is ready even quicker.

350 g (12 oz/1¾ cups) basmati rice
2 tablespoons coconut oil or olive oil
75 g (2½ oz/generous ¾ cup) desiccated (dried shredded) coconut
100 g (2½ oz/generous ½ cup) roasted peanuts
6 spring onions (scallions), finely chopped, white and green parts separated
1 garlic clove, chopped
400 ml (13 fl oz) tin coconut milk
2 tablespoons soy sauce
1 tablespoon miso paste (I like white miso for this)
1 tablespoon light soft brown sugar (or caster (superfine) sugar)
salt and freshly ground black pepper
4 skin-on salmon fillets (about 125 g/4 oz each)
large handful of coriander (cilantro)

A few years back, my friend and now editor, Eve Marleau, wrote a brilliant book, *The Kitchen Shelf*, and this recipe is a new version of the coconut rice and salmon recipe featured in that book. It couldn't be simpler; it remains a stylish little dish that's easy enough for everyday meals, but stunning enough to serve to guests.

———

Rinse the rice under cold running water until the water runs clear. Transfer to a bowl, cover with water and leave to stand for 15 minutes.

Heat half of the oil in a large, shallow, ovenproof casserole dish (Dutch oven) with a lid set over a medium heat. Add the desiccated coconut and peanuts and stir-fry for 2 minutes, or until they are both fragrant and light golden in colour. Spoon out about 3 tablespoons and set aside.

Add the remaining oil to the pan and throw in the white spring onion and garlic. Stir-fry for a minute, or until the rawness has been removed. Drain the rice and add to the pan and fry for 1 minute, stirring to coat in all the ingredients. Pour in the coconut milk, half fill the tin with hot boiled water, then add to the pan with the soy sauce, miso, sugar and some seasoning. Bring to the boil, stirring frequently, and let it bubble gently for 5 minutes.

Season the salmon fillets very well, then place, skin-side down, on top of the rice. Cover the pan with a lid and cook for a further 3 minutes. Turn off the heat and leave to stand, untouched, for 10 minutes.

Gently fluff up the rice around the salmon with a fork, being careful not to break up the fish. Scatter over the reserved toasted coconut and peanuts, the spring onion greens and coriander and serve.

Tip If you don't like peanuts you can change to a nut you prefer, or leave them out, but they do add a lovely crunch.

Oven-baked seafood platter

Serves 4 | Prep 10 minutes | Cook 50 minutes

The Shortcut

When you cook shellfish in a dish with white wine and seasoned butter create the most wonderful sauce. However, make sure you get plenty of sauce inside those shells too, so you can drink it up and enjoy. I blast the corn on the cob for 5 minutes before adding them to the tray to make sure they are perfectly tender when you bite into them.

4 small corn cobettes
1 tablespoon water
75 g (2½ oz) butter, very soft
large handful of flat-leaf parsley, finely chopped
4 garlic cloves, crushed
1 teaspoon garlic salt
1 teaspoon celery salt
1 teaspoon paprika
400 g (14 oz) miniature baby new potatoes, halved if large
4 small or 1 large (200 g/7 oz) smoked cooking chorizo, cut into 3 cm (1¼ in) pieces
12 raw shell-on king prawns (shrimp)
300 g (10½ oz) live mussels, scrubbed clean and beards removed (discard any mussels that are open)
300 g (10½ oz) clams, scrubbed clean
100 ml (3½ fl oz/scant ½ cup) white wine
salt and freshly ground black pepper

Not unlike a seafood boil but I have baked everything in the oven rather than cooking in a seasoned broth. For an easy clean-up after you've eaten, use a paper tablecloth or even old newspaper. Pop some bowls on the table for discarded shells and get stuck in making as much mess as deliciously possible. I love those American seafood dinners where everything is poured onto a plastic sheet-covered table and everybody digs in. This is my version of that, but in an oven dish.

———

Preheat the oven to 200°C fan (400°F/gas 6).

Put the corn on a microwave-safe plate, add the water, cover with cling film (plastic wrap) and microwave on high for 5 minutes. Set aside.

In a small bowl, mix the butter, most of the parsley, the garlic, garlic salt, celery salt and paprika together. Set aside.

Put the potatoes into a 30 x 20 x 5 cm (12 x 8 x 2 in) baking tray (pan), sit the corn on top and add the chorizo in and around. Dollop over a quarter of the butter mixture, cover tightly with foil and cook in the oven for 35 minutes, shaking the pan halfway through.

Remove the tray from the oven and add the prawns, mussels, clams, white wine and the reserved garlic butter mixture. Season really well, stir, then cover with foil again and return to the oven for 12–15 minutes until the shelllfish open and the prawns are piping hot and bright pink. Discard any mussels that do not open. Sprinkle with the reserved parsley and serve immediately.

Tip Discard any damaged mussels and clams. And any that are closed once cooked.

Pork, beef and lamb

Spiced lamb meatballs with couscous, chickpeas and harissa yoghurt

Serves 2 with leftovers | Prep 15 minutes | Cook 15 minutes

The Shortcut

Since couscous only needs to be covered with boiling water, and the lamb meatballs are only bite-size, dinner can be served in just 15 minutes. Mixing the couscous with the meatball cooking juices and some hot stock means none of the flavour is lost.

400 g (14 oz) 20% fat minced (ground) lamb
large handful of mint leaves, finely chopped
large handful of coriander (cilantro), stems and leaves finely chopped
1 teaspoon ground cumin
½ teaspoon ground coriander
1 teaspoon Turkish pepper flakes, plus ½ teaspoon
½ teaspoon ground cinnamon
1 garlic clove, crushed
salt and freshly ground black pepper
1 tablespoon olive oil
½ chicken stock cube
200 ml (7 fl oz/scant 1 cup) boiling water
150 g (5 oz/generous ¾ cup) couscous
400 g (14 oz) tin chickpeas (garbanzos), drained
8 dried apricots, roughly chopped (optional)
handful of toasted flaked (slivered) almonds, to serve

For the harissa yoghurt
200 g (7 oz) Greek-style yoghurt
2 tablespoons rose harissa
½ garlic clove, crushed

This is one of those recipes where cooking it in the one pan harnesses all the flavours from the juicy meatballs, which make the couscous so tasty as the grains soak them up as they cook. I love serving this with some harissa yoghurt, but a dollop of good yoghurt mixed with garlic would also work, as well as a chopped salad. The apricots are optional, but their little pop of sweetness works well with the meatballs.

———

In a large bowl, mix the minced lamb, most of the mint and coriander, the dried spices, garlic and plenty of salt and pepper together, squelching the meat between your fingers for a minute or so to fully combine and distribute all of the flavours. Divide the meat into four pieces, then divide each piece into four small walnut-size balls to make 16.

Preheat the oven to 180°C fan (350°F/gas 4). Heat the olive oil in a 30 x 20 x 5 cm (12 x 8 x 2 in) baking tray (pan) in the oven for a few minutes

Remove the tray and carefully add the meatballs to the hot oil. Cook in the oven for 10 minutes.

Meanwhile, put the stock cube into a measuring jug with the extra ½ teaspoon of pepper flakes and plenty of seasoning. Add the boiling water and stir to dissolve the stock cube.

Remove the meatballs from the oven, add the couscous, chickpeas and dried apricots (if using). Pour over the boiling stock, stir and bring the meatballs back to the surface. Return to the oven and cook for 5 minutes.

Meanwhile, for the harissa yoghurt, mix the yoghurt, harissa and garlic together in a bowl.

Serve the meatballs and couscous scattered with the reserved chopped herbs, toasted flaked almonds and a dollop of harissa yoghurt.

Tip Minced (ground) beef also works if you don't have lamb.

Beef stew with cheesy dumplings

Serves 4 | Prep 20 minutes | Cook 45 minutes

The Shortcut

Making dumplings is super easy, just use your box grater to get the butter uniformly shredded, then it's a quick mix and roll to dumpling heaven. The dumplings are cooked right on top of the hot stew so their bases soak up the rich juices while the tops crisp up. I just give my root vegetables a scrub and a wash; I don't bother peeling them unless they're very gnarly.

1 tablespoon olive oil
1 onion, chopped
2 carrots, chopped
2 celery stalks, chopped
1 parsnip, chopped
500 g (1 lb 2 oz) 20% fat minced
   (ground) beef
1 tablespoon miso paste
1 tablespoon soy sauce
1 tablespoon fish sauce
1 tablespoon Worcestershire sauce
2 tablespoon tomato purée (paste)
1 tablespoon flour (self-raising is
   fine; it won't hurt the stew!)
2 tablespoons thyme leaves or
   1 teaspoon dried thyme
1 fresh or dried bay leaf
1 stock cube
600 ml (20 fl oz/2½ cups) boiling
   water
green cabbage, to serve (optional)

For the cheese dumplings

200 g (7 oz/1⅔ cups) self-raising
   flour
100 g (3½ oz) very cold butter (I pop
   it in the freezer for 15 minutes)
100 g (3½ oz) strong Cheddar,
   coarsely grated
1 tablespoon thyme leaves, chopped
100–125 ml (3½–4 fl oz/scant ½ cup
   –½ cup) milk

I've called this a stew but it's really a deliciously rich base of a great cottage or beef pie, all served here with soft, fluffy cheesy dumplings baked on top of it. This is comfort food at its best. It looks traditional, but I've added a few special ingredients which I add to stews to boost the flavour – miso paste, soy sauce and, of course, fish sauce, the flavour triplets! You won't notice them individually but together they provide the umami depth you get from slow cooking meat. Try it, I know you'll love it.

———

Heat the olive oil in a large, shallow, ovenproof casserole dish (Dutch oven). Add the onion, carrots, celery and parsnip and fry over a medium-high heat for 5 minutes. Push the veg to one side, increase the heat and add the beef. Leave untouched for 2 minutes to brown, then break up the meat with a wooden spoon and cook for 3 minutes, or until browned all over.

Add the miso, soy sauce, fish sauce, Worcestershire sauce and tomato purée to the mince, stir in the flour and cook for 1 minute. Add the thyme, bay leaf and crumble in the stock cube. Pour in the boiling water. Bring to a simmer, then reduce the heat and cook for 10 minutes.

Preheat the oven to 180°C fan (350°F/gas 4).

To make the dumplings, add the flour to a large bowl. Using the coarse edge of a box grater, grate the butter on top of the flour, then stir with your fingers to incorporate, pinching the mixture so the flour sticks to the butter. Add three-quarters of the cheese and the thyme, then add the milk and quickly combine with a butter knife until you have a soft dough. Bring the dough together on a board, then divide into eight pieces. Divide each piece in half so you have 16 small balls.

Flatten the balls lightly then arrange on top of the stew. Scatter each dumpling with a little of the remaining cheese. Bake in the oven, uncovered, for 25 minutes, or until the dumplings are doubled in size and golden. Serve immediately with green cabbage, if you like.

Lamb doner kebab with garlic sauce and shredded salad

Serves 4 | Prep 14 minutes | Cook 40 minutes, plus cooling

The Shortcut

Adding a little bicarbonate of soda (baking soda) stops the meat producing too much liquid; it also keeps it juicy and tender as well as helping to achieve a rich brown colour on the surface.

500 g (1 lb 2 oz) 20% fat minced (ground) lamb
1 onion, coarsely grated
2 garlic cloves, grated
¼ teaspoon bicarbonate of soda (baking soda)
1 tablespoon water
2 teaspoons ground coriander
2 teaspoons ground cumin
2 teaspoons paprika
1 teaspoon dried oregano
1 teaspoon garlic salt
salt and freshly ground black pepper

For the shredded salad
½ red cabbage, shredded
1 small red onion, sliced
2 carrots, coarsely grated
handful of flat-leaf parsley, finely chopped

For the garlic sauce
150 g (5 oz) plain yoghurt
4 tablespoons mayonnaise
2 garlic cloves, crushed
juice of ½ lemon and other ½ cut into wedges, to serve
salt

To serve
pitta bread or wraps
chopped tomatoes, cucumber and shredded lettuce
pickled chillies
chilli sauce

I love a doner kebab, thinly sliced, spiced lamb meat piled into a toasted pitta bread with loads of salads and sauces – absolute heaven. The best thing about my doner kebab is that you get to eat it while it's still hot and pick and choose your favourite salads. I always use a mix of bits and bobs to go with my doners, such as my favourite shop-bought hummus, loads of pickles, some good oven French fries and, of course, a stack of paper towels.

———

Preheat the oven to 160°C fan (325°F/gas 3).

Put the lamb, onion, garlic, bicarbonate of soda and water into a large bowl. Add the spices and plenty of seasoning and work the mixture for 5 minutes to really break down the fibres of the meat and to fully combine and distribute all of the flavours.

Lay a large piece of foil over a large 39 x 27 x 2 cm (15½ x 10¾ x ¾ in) baking tray (pan). Roll the meat into a 22 x 8 cm (8½ x 3¼ in) sausage shape, wrap the foil up around it and seal the edges. Cook in the oven for 35 minutes. Remove from the oven and leave to rest for 10 minutes.

Meanwhile, to make the shredded salad, put the cabbage, onion and carrot into a large bowl and sprinkle with salt. Set aside. To make the garlic sauce, mix all the ingredients together with some salt in another bowl. Cover and chill until required.

Unwrap the meat and transfer to a cutting board. Lay the foil out flat again in the tray, discard any juices (if you can, salvage the foil; use new if not).

Preheat the grill (broiler) to high. Use a sharp knife to thinly slice the doner meat, back on the tray and flash under the hot grill for 1–2 minutes until crisp and charred in places.

Mix the parsley into the shredded salad. Heat some pitta bread or wraps, and pile in the shredded salad, garlic sauce, salad and slices of meat. Alternatively, just pile the ingredients on to the pitta, enjoy with pickles and your favourite chilli sauce.

My moussaka

Serves 4 | Prep 20 minutes, plus cooling | Cook 50 minutes

The Shortcut

A short blast in the microwave cooks the potatoes. No béchamel here; I make a rich, yoghurt and egg-based white sauce, which is perfectly creamy and saves so much time not to mention washing-up, compared to the traditional béchamel.

This is a beautiful light version of a classic Greek dish. Rather than layer the ingredients, I cook the aubergines (eggplants) into the meat, as they soak up all the flavours and make for the most luxurious meat layer with silky aubergine. My version of a béchamel calls for Greek yoghurt, but make sure you use whole (full-fat), not only for its deliciously creamy flavour, but for its fat content so it doesn't split during cooking, which can happen with its low-fat counterparts.

---

3 large potatoes, left whole
3 tablespoons olive oil, plus extra
    for drizzling
2 aubergines (eggplants), cut into
    2 cm (¾ in) dice
salt and freshly ground black
    pepper
500 g (1 lb 2 oz) 20% fat minced
    (ground) beef or lamb
1 onion, grated
1 carrot, grated
2 teaspoons dried oregano
2 bay leaves
1 teaspoon ground cinnamon
400 g (14 oz) tin finely chopped
    tomatoes
1 beef stock cube
300 ml (10 fl oz/1¼ cups) water
2 tablespoon tomato purée (paste)
1–2 teaspoons red wine vinegar
salad, to serve

For the topping
400 g (14 oz) whole (full-fat)
    Greek yoghurt
2 eggs
100 ml (3½ fl oz/scant ½ cup)
    double (heavy) cream, plus
    2 tablespoons
freshly grated nutmeg
100 g (3½ oz) grated mozzarella
    and Cheddar mix

Prick the potatoes all over with a fork and cook on a microwave-safe plate in the microwave on high power for 10–15 minutes until tender. Leave to cool for about 10 minutes, then when cool enough to handle, cut into 5 mm (¼ in) thick slices.

Meanwhile, heat the olive oil in a large, shallow, ovenproof casserole dish (Dutch oven). Add the aubergines sprinkle with 1 teaspoon of salt and fry for 10 minutes, stirring every minute or so to stop them from sticking. Transfer the aubergines to a bowl.

Add a drizzle more oil to the pan, then add the meat, grated onion, carrot and herbs and cinnamon and fry for 5 minutes, or until browned. Add the tinned tomatoes, stock cube and water and bring to a simmer. Squeeze in the tomato purée and add a little vinegar and seasoning. Return the aubergine to the dish and add the extra 2 tablespoons of cream. Cook for 5 minutes.

Preheat the oven to 180°C fan (350°F/gas 4).

To make the topping, in a large bowl, mix together the yoghurt, eggs and cream with plenty of seasoning and a good grating of fresh nutmeg until smooth. Arrange the potatoes in a layer on top of the meat, spoon over the creamy yoghurt topping and sprinkle with the grated cheese. Bake for 20–25 minutes until golden. Serve with a big salad.

Pepper, sausage and mozzarella bake

Serves 4 | Prep 15 minutes | Cook 50 minutes

The Shortcut

If you want all the delicious flavours and textures of a pizza but don't want to make the dough or order a takeaway (take-out) then try this recipe. Tearing up ciabatta into chunks means you get some gooey pieces, some crispy pieces and the creamy mozzarella holds everything together just like a delicious pizza.

4 tablespoons olive oil
1 teaspoon fennel seeds
½ teaspoon chilli (hot pepper) flakes
1 teaspoon flaky sea salt
4 long pointed red peppers, halved lengthways and deseeded
1 red onion, cut into 8 wedges
8 good-quality pork cocktail sausages
250 g (9 oz) vine-ripened cherry tomatoes, halved
handful of black kalamata olives
1 tablespoon capers
2 ciabatta rolls, torn into bite-size pieces
125 g (4 oz) mozzarella, drained and torn into bite-size pieces
large handful of basil, to serve

This recipe is a take on those delicious Italian sausage and slow-cooked pepper rolls combined with a cheesy pizza with sausage. All the complementary flavours meld together gorgeously and the crispy chunks of ciabatta stay crisp and oily on top and gooey and juicy on the bottom where they soak up the juices. This is a family favourite, so try it. I'm sure you'll love it too.

———

Preheat the oven to 200°C fan (400°F/gas 6) and lightly grease a large 39 x 27 x 2 cm (15½ x 10¾ x ¾ in) baking tray (pan) with a little olive oil.

Crush the fennel seeds, chilli flakes and flaky salt in a mortar with a pestle until it is a coarse powder. Add the peppers and onion wedges to the prepared tray. Drizzle with the olive oil and sprinkle with the spice mix, then toss everything together. Sit the sausages on top and cook in the oven for 25 minutes.

Remove the sausages from the oven, add the tomato halves, olives, capers and ciabatta pieces and return to the oven for 10 minutes.

Remove the tray from the oven, turn some of the bread over to expose the uncooked side and push some of the crunchier pieces into the pan juices. Scatter over the mozzarella and return to the oven for a further 10 minutes, or until the ciabatta is crisp and the mozzarella melted. Scatter with basil before serving.

Swedish-style meatballs with creamy gravy

Serves 4 | Prep 20 minutes, plus chilling | Cook 20 minutes

The Shortcut

The creamy gravy for the meatballs is made directly in the pan that the meatballs are cooked in. Don't waste any of that flavour you've built up in the pan – it makes the perfect base for your gravy.

75 g (2½ oz/scant 1 cup) fresh breadcrumbs
1 onion, coarsely grated
2 tablespoons milk
250 g (9 oz) 20% fat minced (ground) beef
250 g (9 oz) 5% fat minced (ground) pork
¼ teaspoon ground allspice
¼ teaspoon freshly grated nutmeg
handful of dill, leaves picked and finely chopped
salt and freshly ground black pepper
olive oil, for cooking
1 tablespoon butter
1 heaped tablespoon plain (all-purpose) flour
500 ml (17 fl oz/2 cups) good-quality beef stock (I buy the stock in pouches for this)
50 ml (1¾ fl oz/3 tablespoons) double (heavy) cream
1 teaspoon Dijon mustard

To serve
oven-cook French chips (fries) or mashed potato
lingonberry sauce or cranberry sauce

These juicy little pork meatballs are totally addictive and so simple to make. The creamy gravy is just begging to be mopped up with hot chips (fries) or spooned into your mouth with a dollop of mashed potato.

———

Put the breadcrumbs, grated onion and milk into a large bowl and leave to stand for a few minutes until the breadcrumbs have absorbed the milk. Add the meat, spices and most of the dill and season really well. Use your hand to massage the meat thoroughly for about 3 minutes. This will stop it falling apart when it is cooked. Form the mixture into 16 small walnut-size balls and chill in the refrigerator for 15 minutes.

Heat a drizzle of olive oil in a large, shallow frying pan (skillet) or shallow, ovenproof casserole dish (Dutch oven) over a medium heat and fry the meatballs for 5–8 minutes, turning frequently until golden. Push the meatballs to one side, add the butter and flour and stir until a paste forms. Gradually add the beef stock and stir until smooth. Redistribute the meatballs into the sauce and cook for 10 minutes, turning the meatballs in the sauce every few minutes, or until the sauce has reduced slightly and is a little thicker and the meatballs are cooked through.

Stir in the cream and mustard and let it bubble for a few minutes. Remove from the heat and serve scattered with the remaining dill and with some fries or creamy mash and a dollop of lingonberry or cranberry sauce.

Tip You can easily double this recipe and fry the meatballs, then leave them to cool and freeze in batches. When ready to cook, defrost and make the gravy in the pan once the meatballs have defrosted.

Sausage, lentil and apple bake

Serves 4 | Prep 15 minutes | Cook 45 minutes

The Shortcut

I use a pouch of ready-to-eat lentils, as these are a lifesaver for hearty meals like this when you just don't have the time or inclination to cook dried lentils. Adding a splash of cider vinegar to apple recipes really brings out their delicious fruity flavour.

2 small onions, cut into wedges through the root
½ teaspoon chilli (hot pepper) flakes
1 tablespoon olive oil, plus extra for rubbing
salt and freshly ground black pepper
8 good-quality sausages (pork or chicken work well)
1 stock cube in 200 ml (7 fl oz/ scant 1 cup) boiling water
200 ml (7fl oz/scant 1 cup) cider or apple juice
1 teaspoon wholegrain mustard
1 tablespoon Dijon mustard
1 apple, cored and sliced
250 g (9 oz) pouch ready-to-eat Puy lentils
1–2 teaspoons cider vinegar, to taste
handful of flat-leaf parsley, chopped (optional)

This is a great all-year-round dish; the apples and cider make it beautiful and warming for autumn and winter, but equally bright enough for spring and summer. In winter I like to serve it with some bread and in summer, a hearty green salad with plenty of fennel and more apple. Even if you are only cooking for one or two people, I urge you to make this one as the leftovers are even better.

———

Preheat the oven to 220°C fan (425°F/gas 7).

Add the onion wedges and chilli flakes to a 30 x 20 x 5 cm (12 x 8 x 2 in) baking tray (pan), drizzle over the olive oil, season with salt and pepper and toss to coat. Sit the sausages on top, rubbing each one with a little olive oil. Bake for 20 minutes until golden on top.

Meanwhile, in a measuring jug, dissolve the stock cube in the boiling water. Add the cider and both mustards and stir to combine.

Remove the sausage and onion from the oven, turn the sausages over and prick with a fork, then return them to their original position (golden-side up). Pour in the stock and cider mixture, add the sliced apple and lentils, give it a gentle stir to combine and cook for a further 25 minutes.

Taste for seasoning and add a little cider vinegar to brighten and bring out the apple flavour. Scatter with chopped parsley before serving, if you like.

Pork tenderloin, braised fennel and butter beans with salsa verde

Serves 4 | Prep 20 minutes | Cook 40 minutes

The Shortcut

Pork tenderloin (fillet) cooks in a fraction of the time it would take a joint of pork to cook. Since the tenderloin doesn't come with crackling, I buy a bag of pork scratchings and crush them up and then sprinkle them over at the end.

2 small onions, cut into wedges through the root
1 large or 2 small fennel bulbs, cut into 1 cm (½ in) wide wedges, fronds reserved
4 tablespoons olive oil
salt and freshly ground black pepper
500 g (1 lb 2 oz) pork tenderloin (fillet), trimmed of any sinew
2 teaspoons Dijon mustard
2 teaspoons fennel seeds
½ teaspoon chilli (hot pepper) flakes
½ teaspoon dried oregano
30 g (1 oz) packet flat-leaf parsley, roughly chopped
grated zest and juice of 1 lemon
1 chicken stock cube
200 ml (7 fl oz/scant 1 cup) boiling water
200 g (7 oz) vine-ripened cherry tomatoes, halved
400 g (14 oz) tin butter (lima) beans, drained
1 garlic clove, chopped
4 anchovy fillets in oil
1 tablespoon capers, drained
40 g (1½ oz) bag pork scratchings, crushed (optional), to serve

My timings for this are tried and tested and will result in juicy slices of roasted pork. The salsa verde adds a depth of flavour to the dish and brings out the sweet roasted vegetables and lean, juicy pork. I love this one! The salsa verde will keep in the refrigerator covered for a couple of days.

———

Preheat the oven to 180°C fan (350°F/gas 4).

Add the onion and fennel wedges to a 30 x 20 x 5 cm (12 x 8 x 2 in) baking tray (pan), drizzle over 1 tablespoon of the olive oil, season well, then toss the vegetables to coat. Lay the pork on top of the vegetables, and spread 1 teaspoon of mustard onto the top and sides of the pork.

Crush the spices, dried oregano and ½ teaspoon of salt in a mortar with a pestle until it is a coarse powder. Add about 2 tablespoons of chopped parsley and half of the lemon zest and bash to mix. Rub half of this spice mix over the pork, making sure to cover the surface, pushing it in with your fingers to ensure it sticks. Gently turn the pork over and spread the surface with the remaining mustard, then spread the rest of the herb and spice mixture over the top. Cook in the oven for 30 minutes.

In a measuring jug, dissolve the stock cube in the boiling water. Remove the tray from the oven, add the cherry tomatoes, butter beans and the hot stock, then return to the oven and cook for 10 minutes.

Meanwhile, for the salsa verde, put the remaining parsley on a cutting board with the remaining lemon zest, chopped garlic, anchovies and capers and chop very finely. Scrape into a bowl and add the remaining 3 tablespoons of olive oil and the lemon juice.

Once the pork is cooked, lift onto a cutting board and cut into 1 cm (½ in) thick slices. Stir a couple of tablespoons of salsa verde into the fennel and beans, then spoon these onto plates and serve with slices of pork, the remaining salsa verde and some crushed pork scratchings, if you like.

Desserts

Gooey lemon bars

Makes 6 | Prep 10 minutes | Cook 40 minutes, plus cooling

The Shortcut

The lemon curd magically makes itself in the oven, so there's no standing over a bain-marie or hot water bath.

85 g (3 oz) butter, at room temperature, plus extra for greasing
2 tablespoons caster (superfine) sugar
100 g (3½ oz/generous ¾ cup) plain (all-purpose) flour
icing (confectioners') sugar, for dusting
salt

For the filling

150 g (5 oz/⅔ cup) caster (superfine) sugar
2 tablespoons plain (all-purpose) flour
2 large eggs
grated zest of 2 large unwaxed lemons
125 ml (4 fl oz/½ cup) lemon juice (from 2–3 large lemons)
salt

If you haven't tried a lemon bar, you really must – rich, buttery shortbread base and that silky lemon custard-curd topping is a match made in heaven. My other half grew up eating these bars and this is a tweak of his favourite Tartine recipe. I've written the recipe to fit into a 900 g (2 lb) loaf pan because they're simply so delicious and addictive that the more you make the more you will eat. They are tart, sweet and gooey in the perfect combination, and to me, they're stylish enough to serve as a dessert with a dollop of good crème fraîche and a handful of raspberries.

_____

Preheat the oven to 180°C fan (350°F/gas 4) and lightly grease and line a 900 g (2 lb) loaf pan with baking parchment.

For the base, add the butter, sugar and flour to a large bowl with a pinch of salt and stir with a wooden spoon until combined. Use your hands to bring the dough together. Tip into the prepared pan and press down evenly to cover the bottom and about 1 cm (¾ in) up the sides of the pan. Bake in the oven for 15–20 minutes until pale golden and smelling enticing.

Meanwhile, for the filling, whisk the sugar, flour, eggs, lemon zest and juice with a pinch of salt together in a large bowl until smooth and there are no lumps of flour.

Remove the pan from the oven and reduce the oven temperature to 160°C fan (325°F/gas 3). Pour the lemon mixture on top of the base, then return to the oven and cook for 20–25 minutes until the lemon custard is set.

Leave to cool completely in the pan, then dust with icing sugar and cut into 6 bars with a sharp knife. Store in an airtight container for 2–3 days in the refrigerator.

Tip Making these in a loaf pan yields the perfect bars. Use a sharp knife to cut the cooled bars really neatly.

Chocolate mousse (it's vegan)

Serves 6 | Prep 15 minutes, plus cooling | Cook 5 minutes

The Shortcut

This is so great eaten slightly warm so you don't even have to wait for it to cool down! Adding cream of tartar to the aquafaba stabilises the mixture and gives the fluffiest meringue-like texture every time.

200 g (7 oz) dark chocolate with at least 72% cocoa solids, roughly chopped
150 ml (5 fl oz/scant ⅔ cup) aquafaba (liquid from 400 g/14 oz tin chickpeas/ garbanzos)
½ teaspoon cream of tartar
100 g (3½ oz/scant ½ cup) caster (superfine) sugar
flaky salt, to serve (optional)

This warm chocolate mousse is so rich and decadent and made with only a handful of ingredients. Amazing on its own, it's also great with crumbled biscuits (cookies) or nuts, spread inside a tart shell or used as icing (frosting) for your favourite cake. You will need an electric hand-held whisk because beating aquafaba (liquid from a tin of beans) is just too hard with a hand whisk.

———

Heat the chocolate in a microwave-safe bowl in the microwave in 20 second bursts until the chocolate has melted. Leave to cool for 5 minutes.

Using an electric hand-held whisk, whisk the aquafaba and cream of tartar in a large bowl for 8 minutes, or until thick and glossy. Add the sugar and beat for a further 2 minutes, or until the sugar has dissolved.

Gently fold through the melted chocolate. Spoon into small serving bowls and eat immediately, sprinkled with a little salt, if you like.

Tip Get to know your aquafaba. Chickpeas usually have more water surrounding them than their white bean counterpart. I used chickpeas for this recipe to ensure I had enough liquid to work with.

Fancy fruit tart

Serves 4–6 | Prep 15 minutes | Cook 20 minutes, plus cooling

The Shortcut

Use ready-made custard instead of making crème patissière. A rolled-out sheet of all-butter puff pastry also saves all that fiddly tart tin (pan) lining.

320 g (11 oz) ready-rolled
    all-butter puff pastry
1 egg yolk, lightly beaten
300 ml (10 fl oz/1¼ cups) double
    (heavy) cream
2 tablespoons caster (superfine)
    sugar
1 teaspoon vanilla extract or
    vanilla bean paste
150 g (5 oz) tub ready-made
    custard
300 g (10½ oz) mixed fruit
    (I used 1 kiwi fruit, sliced
    handful grapes, halved,
    blueberries, raspberries
    and a fresh peach, sliced)

I absolutely love fruit tarts in pâtisseries, laden with fruit and brushed with that characteristic shiny glaze. However, they can often look prettier than they taste, but this tart is just great – delicious crisp pastry, creamy custard filling, piled with your favourite fruit and oh so pretty.

———

Preheat the oven to 180°C fan (350°F/gas 4).

Unroll the pastry sheet and leave it on the paper it comes on. Transfer to a large 39 x 27 x 2 cm (15½ x 10¾ x ¾ in) baking tray (pan) and carefully score a border 1 cm (½ in) from the edge of the pastry. Prick all over the inside of the border with a fork and glaze the border with the beaten egg yolk. Bake in the oven for 15 minutes, or until almost cooked.

Remove the pastry from the oven and push down the centre with the back of a spoon if it has puffed up. Return to the oven and cook for a further 10 minutes. Remove from the oven and leave to cool completely.

Using an electric hand-held whisk, beat the cream, sugar and vanilla together in a large bowl until the cream forms soft peaks when you lift out the whisk, then gently fold through the custard. Spoon this into the centre of the pastry and spread out to the inside edge of the border.

Arrange the fruit on top so it looks beautiful. Cut into squares and serve.

Tip You can cut pastry into small squares, then follow the instructions for scoring a border and baking, then pile with custard cream and top with fruit for an individual afternoon tea offering!

Tiramisu

Serves 6 | Prep 30 minutes | No cook

The Shortcut

I just make a layer of sponge fingers and pour the boozy coffee right over the top as it saves having to soak them and then lift a soggy biscuit (cookie) from one place to another. It also saves on washing-up! I use instant coffee powder, which is easily dissolved.

I've often shied away from making tiramisu believing it to be fiddly and also dangerous to certain groups of people due to the raw eggs. My recipe, however, is not fiddly and it uses aquafaba (the liquid from a tin of beans) whisked up to replace the egg whites. It couldn't be more delicious. I use a mixture of soft brown and caster (superfine) sugar, which gives it the most delicious caramel flavour. Keep the chocolate chunkier for a bit of texture and chocolate hit. Try it!

———

2 tablespoons instant coffee powder, plus ½ teaspoon
250 ml (8½ fl oz/1 cup) boiling water
50 ml (1¾ fl oz/3 tablespoons) coffee liquor or Marsala (or your favourite liquor)
75 g (2½ oz/scant ½ cup) light soft brown sugar, plus 1 tablespoon
150 ml (5 fl oz/scant ⅔ cup) aquafaba (liquid from 400 g/ 14 oz tin chickpeas/garbanzos)
½ teaspoon cream of tartar
50 g (2 oz/scant ¼ cup) caster (superfine) sugar
1 teaspoon vanilla extract
300 ml (10 fl oz/1¼ cups) double (heavy) cream
150 g (5 oz) mascarpone, or other whole (full-fat) cream cheese, stirred to soften
225 g (8 oz) savoiardi sponge fingers
50 g (2 oz) dark chocolate (at least 70% cocoa solids), roughly chopped into shards
2 teaspoons cocoa (unsweetened chocolate) powder

In a measuring jug, mix the 2 tablespoons coffee powder, boiling water, coffee liquor and 1 tablespoon of brown sugar together, then leave to cool.

Using an electric hand-held whisk, whisk the aquafaba and cream of tartar together in a large bowl for 8 minutes until thick and glossy. Tip in the remaining brown sugar and the caster sugar and beat for 2 minutes, or until the sugar has dissolved.

In a small bowl, dissolve the additional ½ teaspoon of coffee powder in the vanilla. Add this to the aquafaba with the cream and mascarpone and beat for 1–2 minutes or until soft, floppy peaks of cream form. Set aside.

Line the base of a 30 x 20 x 5 cm (8 x 12 x 2 in) baking tin (pan) with a layer of savoiardi sponge fingers. Gently pour the coffee mixture over each one covering the entire finger, going back over any parts of the sponge fingers that you haven't covered. You should use about half of the liquid.

Spread half of the cream mixture in an even layer over the sponge fingers. Scatter over half of the chocolate, then dust generously with half of the cocoa. Add another layer of savoiardi fingers. You might have to break a few to make them fit and use any offcuts to fill gaps around the sides. Carefully pour more coffee mixture over each sponge finger making sure that they're well soaked with coffee. Cover them with a layer of cream, scatter over the remaining chocolate and dust with the remaining cocoa. Cover and chill in the refrigerator for at least 2 hours, or overnight.

No-churn strawberry cheesecake ice cream

Serves 8 | Prep 15 minutes, plus freezing | No cook

The Shortcut

Traditional homemade ice cream takes a long time to make as you start with a custard base, which is then chilled and churned. This recipe is so simple and you don't need any fancy equipment. The base freezes in a matter of hours, so there's no pre-chilling or churning required.

100 g (3½ oz) all-butter
    shortbread biscuits (cookies)
100 g (3½ oz) cream cheese
600 ml (20 fl oz/2½ cups) double
    (heavy) cream
397 g (14 oz) tin condensed milk
100 g (3½ oz) soft set strawberry
    jam (I used Bonne Maman)

I love a no-churn ice cream, the base of double (heavy) cream and condensed milk whipped together to stiff peaks can form the basis of all your wildest ice cream dreams. Strawberry cheesecake is one of my favourites but I also love it plain and simple with melted chocolate poured over the top.

———

Put the biscuits into a strong sandwich bag and use a rolling pin to bash to uneven rubble. Drop small nuggets of cream cheese onto the crumbs, turning to coat the cream cheese in the biscuit.

Using an electric hand-held whisk, beat the cream and condensed milk together in a large bowl until soft peaks form, then transfer one-third of the mixture to a 900 g (2 lb) loaf pan.

Drop one-third of the cream cheese biscuit orbs and some crumbs onto the surface of the cream and spoon over a few dollops of strawberry jam. Use a spoon to ripple through it slightly. Cover with another layer of the whipped cream mixture. Repeat with another third of the biscuit, plus some crumbs, cream cheese and jam and then repeat again until all the ingredients have been used up. Cover with cling film (plastic wrap) or foil and freeze for at least 3 hours. Scoop and serve. Freeze any leftovers for up to a month.

Chocolate orange self-saucing pudding

Serves 8 | Prep 40 minutes | Cook 30 minutes

The Shortcut

A pudding where the sauce makes itself during the baking is my kind of dessert.

If you haven't made a self-saucing pudding before it can feel like a leap of faith especially when it comes to pouring boiling water mixed with cocoa all over your beautiful cake batter, but believe me, you'll be so impressed with the end result of this super soft sponge and molten chocolate orange sauce.

———

For the cake layer
125 g (4 oz) butter, plus extra
    for greasing
300 g (10½ oz) self-raising flour
1 teaspoon baking powder
150 g (5 oz/⅔ cup) caster
    (superfine) sugar
75 g (2½ oz/⅔ cup) cocoa
    (unsweetened chocolate) powder
grated zest and juice of 1 orange
salt
3 large eggs
150 ml (5 fl oz/scant ⅔ cup) milk
110 g (3¾ oz) milk chocolate orange
    buttons or orange chocolate,
    chopped
pouring cream or vanilla ice
    cream, to serve

For the sauce
100 g (3½ oz/scant ½ cup) caster
    (superfine) sugar
50 g (2 oz/¼ cup) light soft brown
    sugar
50 g (2 oz/scant ½ cup) cocoa
    (unsweetened chocolate) powder
50 ml (1¾ fl oz/3 tablespoons)
    orange juice (from 1 large
    orange)
250 ml (8½ fl oz/1 cup) boiling
    water

Preheat oven to 160°C fan (325°F/gas 3) and grease a 30 x 20 x 5 cm (8 x 12 x 2 in) baking tin (pan).

Heat the butter in a microwave-safe bowl in the microwave in bursts of 10 seconds until melted. Leave to cool for a few minutes.

Add the flour, baking powder, caster sugar, cocoa, orange zest and a pinch of salt to a large bowl. Pour the orange juice into the cooled butter and crack the eggs in. Add the milk and stir to combine.

Pour the wet ingredients into the dry ingredients and mix everything together until smooth. Fold through the orange chocolate, then scrape the mixture into the prepared tin.

For the sauce, in a large heatproof bowl, mix all the ingredients together and pour this over the batter. Bake in the oven for 30 minutes until the top is risen and firm. Have faith there is a pool of molten sauce under the sponge. Serve immediately with chilled cream or ice cream.

Big batch chocolate chip cookies

Makes 22 | Prep 15 minutes | Cook 12–15 minutes, plus cooling

The Shortcut

For the same amount of effort that you'd put into making a batch of cookies you can have multiple batches – perfect for any occasion.

150 g (5 oz) butter
250 g (9 oz/2 cups) plain (all-purpose) flour
1 teaspoon bicarbonate of soda (baking soda)
½ teaspoon flaky salt, plus extra to serve
125 g (4 oz/⅔ cup) light soft brown sugar
75 g (2½ oz/⅓ cup) caster (superfine) sugar
1 large egg
2 teaspoons vanilla extract
200 g (7 oz) chocolate chunks (I use a mix of white and dark)
85 g (3 oz/generous ¾ cup) toasted pecans, roughly chopped

Hands up if you're always in the mood for chocolate chip cookies. Me too! I love this recipe as it yields enough cookie dough to bake some straight away and some for later, too. It's the gift your future self will thank you for. I can imagine how I feel once these warm, chewy, crisp, chocolatey cookies are just baked and filling the house with their delicious smell. Pure bliss.

_____

Preheat oven to 160°C fan (325°F/gas 3) and line a large baking tray (pan), about 39 x 27 x 2 cm (15½ x 10¾ x ¾ in), with baking parchment.

Melt the butter in a microwave-safe bowl in the microwave in 10 second blasts. It should take about 30 seconds. Leave to cool for about 10 minutes.

In a large bowl, mix together the flour, bicarbonate of soda, salt and both types of sugar thoroughly. Make a well in the centre.

Crack the egg into the cooled butter, then add the vanilla and stir to combine. Pour this mixture into the well of the dry ingredients and mix until there are no traces of dry flour.

Quickly fold in the chocolate chunks and pecans until evenly distributed. Scoop out six golf ball-size cookie dough balls (about 40 g/1½ oz each) and spread them out on the prepared tray, leaving about 5 cm (2 in) between each cookie. Sprinkle with extra salt and bake in the oven for 12 minutes, or until they are golden brown at the edges with a slightly soft centre. Remove from the oven and leave to cool on the tray.

Meanwhile, continue to roll the remaining dough into balls, lay out on a prepared tray, then transfer to the refrigerator to chill for about 1 hour. Once the cookie dough is really firm, pop into freezer-proof bags and freeze for up to 3 months.

Tip To cook the dough balls from frozen, place on a lined baking tray (pan) and bake as above, allowing an extra 3 minutes. If you don't like pecan nuts, swap them out for your favourite alternative or leave them out altogether – I love the slightly savoury crunch they bring to the cookie.

Classic sponge cake

Makes 12 squares | Prep 15 minutes | Cook 35 minutes

The Shortcut

Baking margarine is inherently soft so you don't have to wait for it to soften. My favourite is Stork. It also makes the texture just so fluffy and light. I have converted many a diehard butter fan to its brilliance in cakes, so you can trust me.

This is my most versatile cake recipe ever. I use it for so many things... school dinner cake iced (frosted) and covered in sprinkles, topped with softly whipped cream and macerated strawberries for a strawberry shortcake, or cut in half and sandwiched with raspberry jam and softly whipped cream for a classic Victoria sponge sandwich cake.

_____

The strawberry shortcake version is photographed on back cover

200 g (7 oz) baking margarine (I use Stork), plus extra for greasing
200 g (7 oz/scant 1 cup) caster (superfine) sugar
2 large eggs
100 g (3½ oz) plain yoghurt
2 teaspoons vanilla extract
200 g (7 oz/1⅔ cups) self-raising flour

For the sprinkle topping (optional)
200 g (7 oz/1⅔ cups) icing (confectioners') sugar, sifted
1–2 tablespoons water
food colouring (optional)
sprinkles

For the strawberry shortcake (optional)
350 g (12 oz) strawberries, hulled and sliced
3 tablespoons caster (superfine) sugar
squeeze of lemon juice
300 ml (10 fl oz/1¼ cups) double (heavy) cream

Preheat the oven to 160°C fan (325°F/gas 3) and grease and line a 30 x 20 x 5 cm (12 x 8 x 2 in) baking tin (pan) with baking parchment.

Using a wooden spoon, beat the margarine and sugar together in a large bowl until pale and creamy. Add the eggs, yoghurt and vanilla and beat for a few seconds to incorporate. Add the flour and beat again until it is a smooth, thick batter.

Transfer the batter to the prepared tin and smooth out into an even layer. Bake in the oven for 40–45 minutes until a skewer inserted into the centre comes out clean. Leave to cool for 10 minutes in the tin, then turn out on to a wire rack and cool completely.

If making the sprinkle topping, in a large bowl, mix the icing sugar, water and some food colouring (if using) together until it is a smooth, thick icing. Spread all over the surface of the cooled cake, cover with sprinkles and leave to set before cutting into squares and serving.

If making the strawberry shortcake topping, add the sliced strawberries, sugar and a squeeze of lemon juice to a large bowl and toss until the strawberries are coated in the sugar mixture. Leave to stand while the cake is cooling, as they will become juicy and syrupy. Whip the cream to soft peaks. Once the cake has cooled, spoon over some of the syrupy strawberry juices, spread the cake with the cream, then arrange the sliced strawberries on top. Cut into squares and serve with any extra strawberry juices spooned over. Store any leftovers in an airtight container for 2–3 days in the refrigerator.

Sticky roast pineapple with coconut mango soft serve

Serves 4–6 | **Prep 15 minutes** | **Cook 15 minutes**

The Shortcut

I often use frozen cubes of pineapple or tinned pineapple in juice, drained. Roasting intensifies the natural sweetness of the fruit and using tinned or frozen means you don't have to prep the pineapple.

I love the combination of hot and cold. This sticky roasted pineapple and super-fast soft serve ice cream is so easy to whip up but still manages to feel considered. Aside from the taste the best thing about it is its universal appeal. Young babies, children and adults love this one and I have been known to add a little drop or two of dark rum into the syrupy juices for the grown-ups.

———

25 g (1 oz) butter
500 g (1 lb 2 oz) frozen pineapple chunks, defrosted or a small pineapple, peeled and chopped
6 tablespoons light soft brown sugar
pinch of ground cinnamon
pinch cayenne pepper
grated zest and juice of 2 limes
2 tablespoons water

For the soft serve ice cream
500 g (1 lb 2 oz) frozen mango
350 g (12 oz) plain coconut yoghurt
2 tablespoons maple syrup
toasted coconut flakes, to serve (optional)

Preheat the oven to 180°C fan (350°F/gas 4).

Heat the butter in a 30 x 20 x 5 cm (12 x 8 x 2 in) baking tin (pan) in the oven for 3 minutes until melted. Add the pineapple chunks, sugar, spices, lime juice and water. Stir then cook in the oven for 15 minutes, stirring halfway through and spooning the juices over the pineapple.

Meanwhile, to make the soft serve ice cream, tip the mango into a food processor and pulse a couple of times to chop. Add the yoghurt and maple syrup and whizz until it is smooth, thick and creamy.

Divide the pineapple among plates, top with a scoop of soft serve and scatter over the lime zest and toasted coconut flakes, if using. Drizzle over any sticky juices from the pineapple and serve.

Tip You can make soft serve ice cream with any frozen fruit and yoghurt so play around and find your favourites. You can also make it with Greek-style yoghurt or your favourite vegan yoghurt if you're not into the coconut variety. Freezes well for up to a month.

Index

Acknowledgements

It can be a lonely process writing a cookbook; just me, food and a laptop on repeat! The irony is that there is a big team who all play their part in producing my wonderful books behind the scenes and they all deserve heaps of praise and massive thank yous!

Especially Eila Purvis, Kathy Steer, and an extra special thank you to dear Eve Marleau, for going above and beyond on my behalf and for letting me write another book.

To Nikki Ellis, for your design work and direction on the shoots.

Troy Willis, for being fabulous. You deserve every success that is coming your way.

Jessica Geddes, thank you for all of your hard work and the laughs.

Hannah Wilkinson, for the beautiful props. I love what you have brought to this book.

Clare Winfield, I don't really know where to start my thank yous to you, Clare. It is an absolute pleasure working with you. Calm, considered, a beautiful, funny, naughty, kind human – the best kind!

And finally, Curt, I couldn't do any of this without you and Little Girl cheering me on. For absolutely everything you do for us and for being the best human I know.

Thank you all for helping me produce this beautiful book.

About the Author

Rosie Reynolds is a trained chef, writer and food stylist. She has written cookbooks as well as food styled many best sellers, from Deliciously Ella to Dishoom and many more. Most importantly, Rosie has written as many recipes as she's had hot dinners, with guest columns in *The Sunday Times* and *The Guardian*.

Published in 2023 by Hardie Grant Books,
an imprint of Hardie Grant Publishing

Hardie Grant Books (London)
5th & 6th Floors
52–54 Southwark Street
London SE1 1UN

Hardie Grant Books (Melbourne)
Building 1, 658 Church Street
Richmond, Victoria 3121

hardiegrantbooks.com

British Library Cataloguing-in-Publication Data.
A catalogue record for this book is available from
the British Library.

The Shortcut Cook All in One
ISBN: 978-1-78488-557-1

10 9 8 7 6 5 4 3 2 1

Publishing Director: Kajal Mistry
Acting Publishing Director: Emma Hopkin
Commissioning Editor: Eve Marleau
Senior Editor: Eila Purvis
Design and Art Direction: Nikki Ellis
Photographer: Clare Winfield
Food stylist: Rosie Reynolds
Food stylist assistants: Jessica Geddes
  and Troy Willis
Prop stylist: Hannah Wilkinson
Copy-editor: Kathy Steer
Proofreader: Wendy Hobson
Indexer: Cathy Heath
Production Controller: Sabeena Atchia

Colour reproduction by p2d
Printed and bound in China by Leo Paper
Products Ltd.